IDITAROD
CLASSICS

*Tales of the Trail from
the Men & Women Who Race Across Alaska*

IDITAROD
CLASSICS

Tales of the Trail from
the Men & Women Who Race Across Alaska

By Lew Freedman

Illustrations by Jon Van Zyle

Epicenter Press

Fairbanks/Seattle

Cover design: Leslie Newman, Newman Design/Illustration
Illustrations: Jon Van Zyle
Map: Ed Walker/Leslie Newman
Inside design: Leslie Newman
Typesetting: Stephen Herold, Lasergraphics
Printer: McNaughton & Gunn
Editors: Dermot Cole and Kent Sturgis
Photos: Jeff Schultz, Brian O'Donoghue, Mike Mathers, Sandra Johnson, Nora
Grunner, Eric Muehling, Randy Belinsky, Vladimir Vinitzki, Jim Brown,
Nancy MacRae, with special thanks to Mary Beth Smetzer and Dan Joling of
the Fairbanks Daily News-Miner.
Cover Illustration: "CLOSE CALL" (from 1983 print)
Proofreaders: Stephanie Woolsey, Pat Yockey

Library of Congress Catalog-in-Publication Data

Iditarod Classics: tales of the trail from the men and women who race across
Alaska / [compiled] by Lew Freedman; illustrations by Jon Van Zyle.
    p.   cm.
ISBN 0-945397-11-9 (alk. paper): $16.95 — ISBN)-945397-12-7 (pbk.: alk.
paper): $12.95
     1. Iditarod Trail Sled Dog Race, Alaska. 2. Mushers — Alaska —
Interviews. I. Freedman, Lewis
SF440.15.I35 1992
798′.8—dc20

91-38528
CIP

 This is an Earth-friendly book printed on recycled, acid-free paper, using
non-toxic, soy-based ink. Please share this book.

PRINTED IN THE UNITED STATES OF AMERICA

First printing, February, 1992
Second printing, June, 1992

What the reviewers are saying about IDITAROD CLASSICS:

This collection of first-person accounts of white-outs, frozen equipment, lost sleds and an attack by an enraged moose suggests the Iditarod is best enjoyed from a warm armchair.
— LOS ANGELES TIMES

The mushers' stories are fascinating, something out of another century. You probably wouldn't watch five minutes of this stuff on TV, but you could read about this strange mix of bravado and courage and lunacy all day.
— KNIGHT-RIDDER NEWSPAPERS

This is just the book to send family and friends who are enthralled by the "last great race on earth."
— SITKA (ALASKA) SENTINEL

These nuggets of bravery give readers a feel for the race.
— USA TODAY

IDITAROD CLASSICS is a friendly little book, just like a personal visit with some of Alaska's real characters ... it gives fascinating insight into these people.
— ALL-ALASKA WEEKLY

IDITAROD CLASSICS is a special book. It is as if you gathered all those wonderful Iditarod veterans around a snow-packed campfire and one by one, circled the group and heard their best stories.
— DETROIT FREE PRESS

Just when you thought there wasn't anything new to say about the great Alaskan race, these tales prove you wrong.
— JUNEAU (ALASKA) EMPIRE

DEDICATION

Dedicated to those hardy mushers who have crossed the finish line on Front Street in Nome:

John Ace, Matt Ace, MacGill Adams, Melvin Adkins, Stephen Adkins, Dr. Terry Adkins, Rick Adkinson, Fred Agree, Harold Ahmasuk, Ron Aldrich, Howard Albert, Rose Albert, Dave Allen, Del Allison, Babe Anderson, Eep Anderson, John Nels Anderson, Myron Angstman, Rick Armstrong, Bill Arpino, Gary Attla, George Attla, Jerry Austin;

John Barron, Laird Barron, William Bartlett, Bruce Barton, Lavon Barve, Dick Barnum, Ernie Baumgartner, Henry Beatus, Monique Bene, Francine Bennis, Frank Bettine, Brian Blanford, Guy Blankenship, Marc Boily, Burt Bomhoff, Ed Borden, Rich Bosela, Dennis Boyer, Ralph Bradley, James Brandon, Mitch Brazin, Ron Brennan, Dave Breuer, Bob Bright, Gordon Brinker, Ron Brinker, Frank Brown, Eric Buetow, Richard Burmeister, Richard Burnham, Martin Buser, Steve Bush, Susan Butcher, Paul Byrd;

Scott Cameron, Gary Campen, Chris Camping, Jim Cantor, Gordon Castanza, Bill Cavaney, Ken Chase, Alan Cheshire, Bill Chisholm, Bob Chlupach, Karl Clausen, John Coble, John Coffin, James Cole, Chris Converse, John Cooper, Bill Cotter, Dennis Corrington, Ron Cortte, Dan Cowan, Al Crane;

Tom Dailey, Pat Danly, Bill Davidson, Randy DeKuiper, Billy Demoski, Rudy Demoski, Bruce Denton, Matt Desalernos, Chris Deverill, Diana Dronenburg, Ray Dronenburg;

Neil Eklund, Lars Ekstrand, Ted English, Nikoli Ettyne, Howard Farley, Steve Fee, Stan Ferguson, Linwood Fiedler, Glenn Findlay, Sue Firmin, Charlie Fitka, Stein Havard Fjestad, Steve Flodin, Pam Flowers, Ed Foran, Ed Forstner, Andrew Foxie, Connie Frerichs, Mark Freshwaters, Patty Friend, Peter Fromm, Kevin Fulton;

Steve Gaber, Joe Garnie, John Gartiez, Donna Gentry, Rome Gilman, Jack Goodwin, Ray Gordon, Robert Gould, Ron Gould, Jennifer Gourley, John Gourley, Gary Guy;

Bill Hall, Vern Halter, Duane "Dewey" Halverson, Kathy Halverson, Sandy Hamilton, Ken Hamm, Bert Hanson, Charlie Harrington, Michael Harrington, Larry Harris, Prentice Harris, Steve Haver, William Hayes, Sepp Hermann, Rune Hesthammer, Bob Hickel, Terry Hinesly, Gary Hokkanen, Don Honea, Jack Hooker, Henry Horner, Pecos Humphries, Carl Huntington, Nina Hotvedt, Bob Hoyte, Gordy Hubbard;

Robert Ivan, Owen Ivan, Bill Jack, Clifton Jackson, Ray Jackson, Mark Jackson, Robin Jacobson, Brian Johnson, Bruce Johnson, Gunnar Johnson, Henry Johnson, Ken Johnson, Paul Johnson, Keith Jones, Steve Jones, DeeDee Jonrowe, Victor Jorge;

Peter Kakaruk, Victor Katongan, Desi Kanerer, Rhodi Karella, Walter Kaso, Peter Kelly, Jim Kershner, Armen Khatchikian, Jeff King, Fritz Kirsch, Kazuo Kojima, John Komak, Joel Kottke, Peryll Kyzer;

Duane Lamberts, Ray Lang, Jim Lanier, Calvin Lauwers, Jerry Lavoie, Mike Lawless, Robert Lee, Joe LeFavie, Roger Legaard, Urtha Lenharr, Gene Leonard, Sonny Lindner, Dennis Lozano;

Dan MacEachen, Ian MacKenzie, Darwin MacLeod, Bill Mackey, Dick Mackey, Rick Mackey, Michael Madden, Ralph Mann, Allan Marple, Bob Martin, Jan Masek, Horst Mass, Joe May, Norm McAlpine, Rick McConnel, Don McEwen, Betsy McGuire, Wes McIntyre, Pete McManus, Don McQuown, Lolly Medley, Jerry Mercer, Tom Mercer, Mark Merrill, Allen Miller, Rusty Miller, Terry Miller, Bruce Mitchel, Tim Moerlein, Bryan Molline, Lesley Anne Monk, Roy Monk, Andre Monnier, David Monson, Don Montgomery, Barbara Moore, Marjorie Ann Moore, Don Mormile, Tim Mowry, Larry Munoz;

Herbie Nayokpuk, Jamie Nelson, Peter Nelson, William "Sonny" Nelson, Gayle Nienhauser, Lucy Nordlum, Roger Nordlum, Mark Nordman, Earl Norris;

Brian O'Donoghue, Christine O'Gar, Issac Okleasik, David Olesen, Dave Olson, Red Olson, Dean Osmar, Ron Oviak, Michael Owens;

Dean Painter, John Patten, Gary Paulsen, Steve Peek, Mike Pemberton, Alan Perry, Rod Perry, Kate Persons, Emmitt Peters, Dick Peterson, Mike Peterson, Claire Philip, Jacques Philip, Lynda Plettner, Eric Poole, Shannon Poole;

Jerry Raychel, Joe Redington Sr., Joee Redington Jr., Raymie Redington, Ford Reeves, Ketil Reitan, Darrell Reynolds, Alexandr Reznyuk, Libby Riddles, Steve Rieger, Jerry Riley, Ron Robbins, Roger Roberts, Bill Rose, Mark "Bigfoot" Rosser, Jim Rowe, Joe Runyan, Sonny Russell;

Kevin Saiki, Peter Sapin, Conrad Saussele, Robert Schlentner, Dr. Karin Schmidt, John Schultz, Terry Seaman, Dan Seavey, Mitch Seavey, Reuben Seetot, Richard Self, Leroy Shank, David Sheer, Alex Sheldon, Mike Sherman, Douglas Sherrer, Mary Shields, Clarence Shockley, Tony "Wild Man" Shoogukwruk, Cliff Sisson, Kari Skogen, Caleb Slemons, Jim Smarz, Larry "Cowboy" Smith, Jamie "Bud" Smyth, William Solomon, Brian Stafford, John Stam, Norm Stoppenbrink, Mike Storto, Jim Strong, Jack Studer, John Suter, Mark Suter, Harry Sutherland, Dale Swartzentruber, Rick Swenson;

Rick Tarpey, Frank Teasley, Jon Terhune, Peter Thomann, Conner Thomas, Verona Thompson, Greg Tibbetts, Jim Tofflemire, Frank Torres, Bob Toll, Clarence Towarak, Ron Tucker, Mike Tvenge;

Nathan Underwood, Malcolm Vance, Jon Van Zyle, Shelley Vandiver, Col. Norman Vaughan, Bobby Vent, Warner Vent, Bill Vaudrin, Steve Vollertsen;

Roy Wade, Lorren Weaver, Rollin Westrum, Tim White, Gary Whittemore, Mark Williams, Walter Williams, Bernie Willis, Dick Wilmarth, Frank Winkler, David Wolfe, Jim Wood, John Wood, Roxee Woods;

Bill Yankee, Dan Zobrist, Stan Zuray

...and, of course, to the dogs.

TABLE OF CONTENTS

In 1978, Dick Mackey, then forty-five, won the closest race in Iditarod history, finishing one second ahead of Rick Swensen after mushing more than one-thousand miles. But he best remembers the first race five years earlier.

"You will never be able to duplicate the feeling of the first one. Nobody knew what they were doing. Wives and sweethearts were down at the starting line in tears because here we were going off into the wilds, never to be seen again."

No one paid much attention in 1985 to Libby Riddles, then twenty-eight, until she became the first woman to win the race. Riddles became a legend by driving into a fierce blizzard with gusts to sixty miles per hour after others had turned back.

"It was grim. I could not see from one trail marker to the next. I let my dogs go so far that I could barely see the marker behind me, because I didn't want to lose that sucker. When that was at the edge of my visibility, I'd put my snowhook in and walk up ahead of the dogs until I could see the next marker. And we repeated that process. It was very slow."

Rick Swenson, forty-one, who has run the Iditarod sixteen times and won five times, reflects on changes in one of the world's most unusual sporting events.

"The sled that I won the Iditarod with the first time, I built with hand tools, and I mean non-electric hand tools. Now, people talk about a hand-made sled, they're using a table saw and power drills. I'm talking about hand tools ... It's a different era now. I bet half the people in the top twenty have never built a dogsled using power tools."

Susan Butcher, thirty-seven, a fierce competitor who came back to win the Iditarod four times after an angry moose attacked her team and knocked her out of the race in 1985, gives much credit to a lead dog named Granite.

"The dogs have as much pride as any human athlete. That's why Granite's a wonderful dog. He knows when he's won. He thinks he deserves all the accolades, he expects them. He's a ham in front of the media."

Rick Mackey, thirty-eight, who began sled-dog racing as a teenager in Anchorage, finished first in 1983. He and his father, Dick, are the only father-son winners of the Iditarod.

"When they're looking in the history books years from now my grandkids will say, 'Yeah, that must have been a tough breed, them Mackeys. They had two of them that won it.' That's what makes it special to me."

Martin Buser, thirty-three, placed second in 1991 after chasing Rick Swenson the last seventy-seven miles into Nome

through howling wind, frigid temperatures and blizzard conditions.

"I was dressed for the occasion. It was not cold. Throughout the whole race, I was never cold, other than my face. That's the problem. I had a lot of my face exposed. Every year I get what I call my Norton Sound Facelift. I get a new layer of skin on my face. Instead of getting older, I get younger every time I race."

In 1990, at age eighty-three, Norman Vaughan became the oldest musher to finish the Iditarod. His race, he says, is against himself – and the harsh elements.

"One night was really cold. I was traveling with Steve Haver. We decided we'd better stop, it was so damn cold. I remember I couldn't get in my bag. I was shivering, trying to stay warm. I got into my bag halfway and I couldn't get it up over my shoulders. All my parkas were on, but I was still cold. So we finally yelled to each other, 'Let's go on.' We had forty miles to go before we got somewhere and that was six hours or so."

Joe Redington, seventy-five, is called the Father of the Iditarod for his role in organizing the race in 1973 and helping revive dormant interest in sled dogs in Alaska. That first year, Redington almost single-handedly raised the $50,000 purse for the mushers' prizes.

"I went to banks and they turned me down cold. Some of them said, 'Joe, you're crazy, butting your head against something like that. You don't even know if anybody will get to Nome.' I said, 'Well, they used to get there, why can't we get there again?'"

Duane "Dewey" Halverson, thirty-nine, arrived on the scene with a .44-caliber pistol in 1985 as an angry moose attacked Susan Butcher's team. He shot and killed the moose that forced Butcher and her injured dogs out of the race.

"She didn't have a gun! It was too much weight to carry. That killed me. Everybody felt sorry for her, but it's like running the Iditarod without your parka or harnesses. Whose fault is it, really? I don't feel there's much excuse for it. It wasn't an act of God that she couldn't finish the race that year."

Kathy Halverson, thirty-two, was one of several mushers who gave up their own hopes and dreams halfway through the race to care for Mike Madden, a racer stricken with salmonella poisoning.

"By Unalakleet, we heard Mike was OK. He was at the finish line with tears in his eyes to thank each of the people who helped him out. He knew exactly who had helped him, and he and his father were there and greeted us individually."

Joe Garnie, thirty-eight, lost his dogs during the 1991 race and spent eighteen hours searching for them in a snowstorm. Having grown up at the edge of the wilderness, Garne wasn't

worried about survival, even as he allowed the snow to drift over him while he rested.

"I had stood some pieces of snow up and made a drift. I used my hands. I lay there and let it drift right over me, at least a foot of snow. You want to lay face down, you dig a hole out in front of your face so you've got some air."

Mary Shields, forty-seven, recalls the reaction of some male competitors on the trail in 1974, the year she became the first woman to finish the Iditarod.

"I got the impression that other mushers didn't take me seriously because I was a woman and they didn't particularly want to be seen traveling with me, because that meant they weren't doing so well ... At Shaktoolik, I remember pulling in and a bunch of teams taking off and the checker saying: 'Well, that's strange. They were going to spend the night here, and then you pulled in, and they all took off.' "

Terry Adkins, forty-eight, thought he would make one run in the Iditarod Race in 1974, but he kept coming back again and again – racing seventeen times in all, more than anyone else except Joe Redington.

"The Iditarod grows on you. I want to win it before I quit. I do think if I win I'll quit. There are other enjoyable races — the Alpirod, the John Beargrease — where you can party, sleep in a warm bed and have a hot meal. The Iditarod, you have to work. I kept a log once showing that in thirteen days of racing, I slept nineteen hours."

DeeDee Jonrowe, thirty-seven, has raced nine Iditarods and has vivid memories of the fierce Alaska weather.

"It stormed all up the Yukon River. It was blowing hard enough that if you were a couple hundred feet behind the team in front of you, you were breaking trail again ... We got on the coast and the storms came and the temperatures were very low — thirty, forty below zero and a windchill of nearly one-hundred below. And colder. This is real intense. It's difficult to cook dog food outside, boil water at one-hundred below zero."

Iditarod mushers are a determined bunch. Tim Osmar, twenty-five, a commercial fisherman in summer and a sled-dog racer in winter, first competed in the Iditarod when he was eighteen.

"I've got to win. That would be the turning point in a guy's career, to win the Iditarod. Everything would go well after that. Being able to sell dogs, to get sponsors, to turn a profit. Rick Mackey is still Iditarod champion. It follows you. I know it does. I know I can do it."

Danger is a constant companion on the trail, as Jerry Austin, forty-four, knows well.

"The worst trouble I ever had was when I was up to my neck in water. It was 1976. We went through Ptarmigan Pass. It's the south fork of the Kuskokwim. You just had to walk your dogs through water up to your waist. The sled would be downstream from you. It's cold water, thirty-two degrees. I slipped and was totally soaked ... that is the most miserable I've been and I've got scars and bullet wounds all over my body."

Joe Runyan, forty-three, known as "the thinking man's musher," reflects how the Iditarod has matured as a sporting event.

"In most professional sports you have a draft that evens out the playing field. Certain talent goes to the worst team so they can improve. We don't have that with the Iditarod. You get a dynasty going and it's hard to do well against them. Now, though, with sponsor interest, there are more people with the freedom to do as well as they can. In the next few years, I think it'll be more competitive."

Rudy Demoski, forty-seven, remembers the early days of the Iditarod, before the advent of year-round training and lucra-

tive sponsorships, when a musher from a small village could pull together a team and compete.

"The 1974 Iditarod was the first dog-sled race of my life. My brother-in-law, Ken Chase, raced in 1973 in the first one. It sounded like something I could do. The entry fee was $200 in those days. I trained my dogs in a trap line, trying to get them tough for distance. That's what we all did."

Jon Van Zyle, forty-nine, an internationally known wildlife artist, has a wide following in Alaska for his annual scenes of the Iditarod. In 1979, Van Zyle had an unexplained vision — and heard mysterious whispering, murmuring and laughter — on a lonely stretch of the Yukon River.

"Nobody was there. I wasn't dreaming. I was awake. When I came back I did a painting about it ... A priest told me, 'You're not the first person who's heard these people.' "

ACKNOWLEDGEMENTS

The author would like to thank the many mushers who offered their time and cooperation in the preparation of this book.

A special thanks is due Guy Blankenship, president of the Iditarod Official Finishers Club, an organization of the more than three-hundred mushers who have completed the Iditarod and whose mission is "educating the public about the race in every way possible and improving the care, feeding, training and treatment of the magnificent animals that pull us through this race."

PUBLISHER'S NOTE

A share of the royalties from *Iditarod Classics* will be donated to the Iditarod Official Finishers Club thanks to the generosity of author Lew Freedman, who volunteered to share his royalty with the mushers' organization, and of artist Jon Van Zyle, who waived a royalty in donating the use of his work for this book.

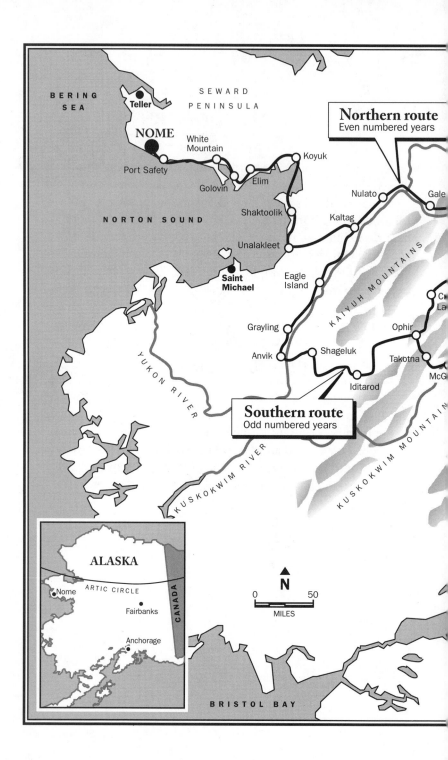

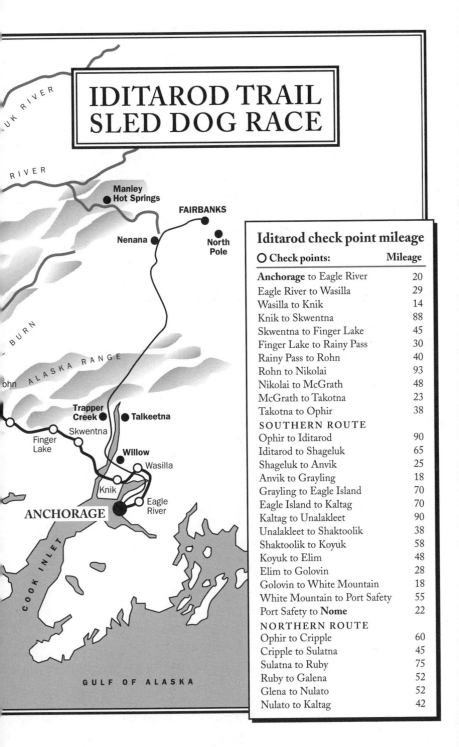

IDITAROD TRAIL SLED DOG RACE

Manley Hot Springs

FAIRBANKS

Nenana

North Pole

ohn

ALASKA RANGE

BURN

Trapper Creek

Talkeetna

Skwentna

Finger Lake

Willow

Wasilla

Knik

ANCHORAGE

Eagle River

COOK INLET

GULF OF ALASKA

Iditarod check point mileage

O Check points:	Mileage
Anchorage to Eagle River	20
Eagle River to Wasilla	29
Wasilla to Knik	14
Knik to Skwentna	88
Skwentna to Finger Lake	45
Finger Lake to Rainy Pass	30
Rainy Pass to Rohn	40
Rohn to Nikolai	93
Nikolai to McGrath	48
McGrath to Takotna	23
Takotna to Ophir	38
SOUTHERN ROUTE	
Ophir to Iditarod	90
Iditarod to Shageluk	65
Shageluk to Anvik	25
Anvik to Grayling	18
Grayling to Eagle Island	70
Eagle Island to Kaltag	70
Kaltag to Unalakleet	90
Unalakleet to Shaktoolik	38
Shaktoolik to Koyuk	58
Koyuk to Elim	48
Elim to Golovin	28
Golovin to White Mountain	18
White Mountain to Port Safety	55
Port Safety to **Nome**	22
NORTHERN ROUTE	
Ophir to Cripple	60
Cripple to Sulatna	45
Sulatna to Ruby	75
Ruby to Galena	52
Glena to Nulato	52
Nulato to Kaltag	42

INTRODUCTION

*A*LL OF US IN ALASKA think of our state in different and personal ways, but somewhere in most of us there is love, an appreciation, an affection, for the land, for the wild, and for the raw beauty of this frontier. It is what drew many of us here, what keeps us here, what makes us Alaskans.

Nothing touches this chord more strongly than sled-dog racing. Something in the sight of the powerful, eager, finely tuned animals mastering the wilderness, touches the romantic in us, expresses so vividly this kinship with the land.

That's why, come March, thousands of us listen for every scrap of information on who is where in the 1,100-mile Iditarod Trail Sled Dog Race from Anchorage to Nome.

The mushers are taming the wilderness for all of us who sit at desks all day, who make our living out of the bitter cold and the brusque elements that rule a state that was never meant to be truly tamed.

We live vicariously through the exploits of the mushers but they, too, even the best of them, share the same emotions, the same excitement, the same thrill, of watching the dogs run. If anything, they feel it more so.

So it is that dog mushers are celebrities in Alaska. Susan Butcher is known by her first name. So is Rick Swenson. And Libby Riddles. Everyone knows who they are.

Since its start in 1973, the Iditarod has evolved from what was essentially a long camping trip, to a highly efficient speed race in which every minute counts. The first Iditarod mushers were out on the poorly defined trail for three weeks, and no one was sure it was possible to run dogs so far. Except perhaps Joe Redington, founder of the race, who somehow scratched together a $50,000 purse for the first one. He always believed.

Now, the fastest mushers are on the trail for barely a week and a half, and they have little time to sleep or enjoy the scenery. The total prize money exceeds $300,000. The Iditarod has become equal parts big business, competition and endurance. Yet it retains the romance of adventure, and the slowest musher takes more than a month to bring home the symbolic red lantern for last place.

The Iditarod owes its origins to the famed diphtheria-serum run of 1925, when Leonhard Seppala and other dog mushers teamed to rush medicine across Interior Alaska from the railroad and river port town of Nenana to the stricken Bering Sea town of Nome in western Alaska.

The race course starts in Anchorage, where thousands of fans line downtown streets to send the mushers off, swerves into the Matanuska-Susitna Valley, cuts through the Alaska Range, then follows an historic path that takes it through tiny Interior villages to Unalakleet on the coast where begins the final all-out run into Nome.

Along the way, mushers and their dogs may encounter bad-tempered moose, dangerous terrain, thin ice, violent storms and paralyzingly cold temperatures.

One major element in the Iditarod hasn't changed: Each year when the race begins, no one knows what new obstacles Alaska will place in front of the mushers.

Sleds and other gear have improved. Dogs are faster. Mushers are better trained. But the weather is just as cold, the wind blows just as fiercely, and the snow falls just as heavily as always.

The mushers interviewed for this collection of stories are a hardy breed. Some were pioneers on the trail, racing twenty years ago when the Iditarod was unknown. Some are champions who have found fame in the race.

What they offer here, in their own words, are tales of the trail — stories of their most challenging moments, their most personal reflections, their candid views on what the Iditarod is and will become.

— Lew Freedman, September, 1991

"FROM WHENCE COME LEGENDS" (1978 poster) *pays tribute to Leonhard Seppala and one of his lead dogs, Scotty.*

CHAMPIONS OF
THE IDITAROD TRAIL
SLED DOG RACE

	TIME	WINNING PURSE
1973 – Dick Wilmarth ...	20 days, 0:49:41,	$12,000
1974 – Carl Huntington .	20 days, 15:02:07,	$12,000
1975 – Emmitt Peters	14 days, 14:43:45,	$15,000
1976 – Jerry Riley	18 days, 22:58:17,	$ 7,200
1977 – Rick Swenson	16 days, 16:27:13,	$ 9,600
1978 – Dick Mackey	14 days, 18:52:24,	$12,000
1979 – Rick Swenson	15 days, 10:37:47,	$12,000
1980 – Joe May	14 days, 7:11:51,	$12,000
1981 – Rick Swenson	12 days, 8:45:02,	$24,000
1982 – Rick Swenson.....	16 days, 4:40:10,	$24,000
1983 – Rick Mackey	12 days, 14:10:44,	$24,000
1984 – Dean Osmar......	12 days, 15:07:33,	$24,000
1985 – Libby Riddles	18 days, 0:20:17,	$50,000
1986 – Susan Butcher....	11 days, 15:06:00,	$50,000
1987 – Susan Butcher	11 days, 2:05:13,	$50,000
1988 – Susan Butcher	11 days, 11:41:40,	$50,000
1989 – Joe Runyan........	11 days, 5:24:34,	$50,000
1990 – Susan Butcher	11 days, 1:53:23,	$50,000
1991 – Rick Swenson	12 days, 16:35:39,	$50,000
1992 – Martin Buser	10 days, 19:17:15,	$51,600

TIME IS LISTED AS DAYS, HOURS: MINUTES: SECONDS

"INTO HELL'S GATE" (1987 print) depicts the head waters of the Kuskokwim River.

Dick Mackey, who moved to Alaska from New Hampshire, helped organize the Iditarod Sled Dog Race after a career in sprint racing.

CHAPTER 1:
DICK MACKEY

*I*DITAROD FANS WERE ASTONISHED in 1978 when Dick Mackey won the closest race in Iditarod history, winning the title in a photo finish with Rick Swenson after the two mushers raced across Alaska for two weeks. At forty-five, Mackey was the oldest race champion.

Mackey's winning time of 14 days, 18 hours, 52 minutes, 24 seconds was one second faster than the time given Swenson for second place. The race was so close that it caused a dispute over the rules. Did the whole team have to cross the finish line? Or just the nose of the lead dog? Officials ruled that only the lead dog must cross.

Mackey was one of the organizers of the first Iditarod in 1973 after a career as a sprint racer. He has homes in Nenana, Alaska, and in Branson, Mo. Dick and his son, Rick, the 1983 winner, are the only father-son combination to win Iditarod championships.

Mackey, who came to Alaska after graduating from high school in Concord, N.H., has lived in many parts of the state, including Anchorage, Wasilla, Nenana and Coldfoot, where he operated a last-chance gas station and lodge for trucks driving north to the Prudhoe Bay oil fields. One winter he says the temperature fell to eighty-two degrees below zero there.

*I*REMEMBER BEFORE THE IDITAROD got started Joe Redington called me and said, "What do you think?" I said, "Well, hell, I'm the second one to sign up." He said, "What do you mean?" I said, "Ain't you signed up yet?" Well, that was in November, 1972, and we went from there.

This idea of a sled-dog race from Anchorge to Nome was a farfetched scheme. It was an adventure that first year. We thought we were racing. But as you look back on it, certainly compared to now, it was a big camping trip.

You never will be able to duplicate the feeling of the first one. Nobody knew what they were doing. Wives and sweethearts were down at the starting line in tears because here we were going off into the wilds, never to be seen again. It was that kind of attitude.

I had fifteen or sixteen dogs that first year. Oh boy, it was a learning process. Everybody went pretty much during the daylight hours. Maybe you'd stretch it a little to get to a certain place, and then you made camp.

Oh man, I was walking ten feet tall at the finish. First didn't make any difference. Everybody was a winner. Dick Wilmarth got there first, that's all. That was the attitude not only of the mushers, but the attitude of the public, too.

Of course there was no idea of doing it a second time. This was a one-time event. To be part of it was … hell's bells, I'd rather have done that than been president of the United States.

There's no doubt it was tough. And those of us that went the second year found out that in some respects the second year was worse.

The weather was atrocious. Hell, a half-dozen of us got trapped there going out of Puntilla Lake. The chill factor was 130 below.

I had a good team every year. I was into the organizational part of the race, though. The first year, I was in the office. I sent out all the information to potential mushers, did all the signing up, took all the money, made all the phone calls.

Finally, in 1978, it dawned on me that the core of my team

was getting a little ancient. I had a damn good dog team and I told myself "I'm going to back off from the organization this year and train dogs."

We went up to Eureka. We went to Talkeetna. We went to Cantwell. Wherever there was snow, we trained, as well as out of my home in Wasilla. I was thinking I had a team capable of winning it. I went into the race with that attitude — that I might not win, but I could keep up with anybody. The "anybody" turned out to be Rick Swenson. He was defending champion. Emmitt Peters, Rick Swenson and I were the top contenders as the race progressed. And Rick and I were the leaders.

Dick Mackey says it was more of a thrill watching his son, Rick, win The Iditarod in 1983 than winning himself.

JEFF SCHULTZ

I let Rick lead. The only time that I was in the lead was where it was easy to be in the lead. When it was difficult to be in the lead I let him lead. Difficult in terms of trailbreaking. He was perfectly content to do that.

Now don't get me wrong. Rick and I are good friends, but at that time in his life he was pretty sure of himself — "I'm the defending champion and you're number two." I was willing to play that game until we got to Nome.

Swenson and I were probably never more than a hundred yards apart for the last eight-hundred miles. We'd go to camp for the night, or however long we were going to camp. He'd get out his cooking stuff and I'd say, "Well, I'm going to go down the trail a little farther." And it would just blow his mind. I was the guy who never took the harness off my dogs. The dogs were always ready to go.

Anyway, this became a head game with Rick. Constantly. He made comments like, "I've never seen anybody who can get ready to go as fast as you can." Or, "I can't lose you for nothin'." And on and on. Well, we got about three miles from Nome and I got my lead dog right between his legs and he turned around to me and says, "We got it made. Just stay right where you are and we'll be first and second." I thought, "Yeah, sure."

As we came up over the sea wall onto Front Street, I reached in my sled bag and pulled out a whip just as he glanced around and saw it. So he reached in and pulled out his. And that's the way we came down the street, just driving those dogs for all there was in us.

He was in front of me and I got in front of him, actually gained about three-hundred feet on him. We both had troubles. I went off onto the sidewalk. He got tangled up with a school bus. He went into the crowd. It was chaotic. Everybody was jumping up and down. And then I got tangled in a camera tripod just as I entered the chute area, and I had to run up front, grab those dogs and pull 'em out. We crossed the finish line just bang-bang, a second apart.

My leaders Skipper and Shrew crossed the finish line and it was a solid mass of people. When his leaders crossed the finish line, Swenson stopped.

I went to fall down in the sled and missed the damn sled. I

had the heavy parka on and I couldn't get the darn thing off. I thought I was going to die from lack of air. Anyway, somebody said, "You gotta cross the line." And I said, "No, you don't." Well, every race you ever ran, you could be running alongside your team, doing anything, when any part of that crossed the finish line, that constituted a finish. You had to be equal to your sled or better. You could pull the sled backwards and be holding onto it, that's OK. With one exception. Nome Kennel Club rules, from way back in the All-Alaska Sweepstakes Race, said team, driver, sled, all had to cross the finish line.

But we weren't running under the Nome Kennel Club rules. They were simply the host club at the finish line in Nome. An official asked Myron Gavin, who was the race marshal that year, "What's your decision?" And it was classic. Myron said, "You don't take a picture of the horse's ass."

Rick was on the back of his sled same as I was. When our leaders crossed, we both stopped. He sat down in his sled and I collapsed into mine.

Tom Bush of KNOM said, "You've got to cross the finish line." They congratulated Swenson, and he said, "For what, coming in second?" Then someone said, "You've got to cross the finish line." So Swenson got up and pushed his sled and himself through the crowd. In the meantime, the race marshal made the determination that as long as anything crosses the finish line, that constitutes a finish.

Swenson and I had equal dog teams and I just out-snookered him into thinking I was willing to be complacent enough to take second. And I wasn't. He learned a lesson.

You know, it was more of a thrill watching my son Rick win the Iditarod in 1983 than my winning. I absolutely went beserk. It is special to be able to say that we are the only father and son so far that have done it. It creates a bond there that you just can't duplicate.

Two teams travel closely together through a Yukon River storm.

Libby Riddles created a legend by driving her dogs into a severe storm that forced other racers back, but says she isn't an Iditarod "lifer."

CHAPTER 2:
LIBBY RIDDLES

*A*T THE STARTING LINE of the 1985 Iditarod no one paid much attention to Libby Riddles, then twenty-eight. She had finished far back in the pack in her two previous races, the first in 1980, and was a virtual unknown.

Yet, Riddles opened a new era in race history that year and created one of the enduring legends of the race by driving her dogs into a severe storm that packed gusts of sixty miles per hour and whiteout conditions that obliterated the trail.

After another musher advised her that it would be impossible to go on, she plunged ahead through the storm and left Shaktoolik to cross Norton Sound. "I allowed only one thought — to keep my lead at all costs, taking it inch by inch if necessary, she wrote later in her book, "Race Across Alaska."

Riddles' daring gamble paid off. She won the race in 18 days, 20 minutes and 17 seconds, six hours faster than her nearest competitor. As the first woman to earn the title of Iditarod champion, she became a national celebrity.

At the time, Riddles lived in Teller on the Seward Peninsula and raised dogs with her partner, Joe Garnie. Since then Riddles has lived on the Nome River, in Banner Creek and in Knik.

I WAS MORE OF A CAT PERSON AS A KID.

The first time I saw dogs in action was in the Fur Rendez-vous in Anchorage. I was just a goner.

If you survive your first year of mushing, especially knowing as little about it as I did, it's amazing that a person would continue. People go to races and they see these nice dog teams all stretched out and doing what they're told to do, and they don't realize what it takes to get a dog team to that point.

When I started, I didn't have any intention of racing at all. I just wanted these dogs so I could haul firewood and haul drinking water so I didn't have to deal with starting a snowmachine, and basically so I didn't have to carry it myself.

I liked the dogs. I liked how much they liked to help me out and work for me and how happy they were pulling a sled. They're happiest when they have a job to do. You treat them right and give them a fair chance and they're just amazing.

I think the Iditarod fit in with what I was already doing — traveling with dogs. I love to go fast, too, but it's a different kind of racing. You can't be running a sprint race against George Attla and Roxy Wright and be looking at the sunset.

I was competitive my first year, in 1980. My objective was to get to Nome in the best fashion that I could. I wasn't going on any camping trip. I was racing. I'm glad that I started the year that I did. It was a horrible year. Half the field scratched. I was too dumb to know any better. I just thought, "It's always like this. What's the big deal?" I was able to finish eighteenth, and I was happy with that.

Winning the race changed my life. It's given me a lot of opportunities and connected me with neat people all over the country. I've met a lot of famous athletes and done lots of traveling.

I knew I had a team that could win. I knew it was a team that was as good as anybody's.

They had two freezes (stoppages) in the race. It was a heavy snow year. That definitely made an impact on the race.

I started with fifteen dogs. I didn't drop one until I got to Unalakleet on the Bering Sea coast. I had sick dogs and during the freezes I concentrated on bringing those dogs back around so I wasn't going to have to drop them. I just babied them. And I stayed among the top five.

When I took the lead it was in a moment of stubbornness. I had rested my dogs on the Yukon. Some guys had a fire going. So I stopped at their fire for about two hours and thawed out. That was around nightfall.

We went on for barely an hour, probably no more than five miles, and here's this Blackburn Lodge and all these dog teams are pulled up in there and there's a fire going, lights on. Looking through the window it looks good, and I was thinking, "Hey, we just took a big rest, we're going to keep on trooping." My dogs tried to go in and join the party. I was halfway thinking, "Hmmm, a cup of coffee might not be bad." But the fact that my dogs went in there without my permission made me feel stubborn. So I said, "C'mon, c'mon, we're going!"

I built a good lead that night because it was so cold that I didn't dare stop. I had to keep moving or freeze my feet. It was forty to fifty below.

It reached the point that if I didn't get in a cabin, or stop and start a fire, I was going to freeze my feet. I was the first one into Eagle Island at about five o'clock that morning.

I got a good twelve-hour rest there and went out the next evening, when it was even colder. It was cold enough that even with a big Eskimo-style fur pullover, the only way I was staying warm going down the trail was with my sleeping bag out, used like a cape around me.

I was sleepy in Unalakleet. I wanted to stay longer than I did. I was dragging, but I got up about five in the morning and booted up the team while it was still dark. I remembered it was so cold I could only put a few booties on and then had to thaw my hands.

It was a long forty miles to Shaktoolik.

I got there about one in the afternoon. It was blowing like hell. The weather three hours later when I left was worse.

I was nervous because I was in first place and wanted to stay there. The weather was not anything I wanted to travel in, and if

I would have been at home I would never have dreamed of traveling in it, to tell you the truth. But it's different when you're in a race.

Still, having lived in that country for quite a few years, I think I had an awareness of how dangerous it could be. When it came time to get going, I didn't really think. I just did it.

Lavon Barve was rolling in as I was packing my sled and getting ready to go. He came over, shaking his head, and couldn't believe it because he'd just been battered out there. He said something like, "You're crazy if it's like what I just came through." In a way that gave me even more incentive. I knew it was a little crazy. I knew it was more than a little crazy, actually.

And it was bad. I couldn't believe I was there. Part of what you get from dog mushing is patience. Patience, I think, was the calming factor when I was out in this storm.

It was grim. I could not see from one trail marker to the next. I let my dogs go so far that I could barely see the marker behind me, because I didn't want to lose that sucker. When that was at the edge of my visibility, I'd put my snowhook in and walk up ahead of the dogs until I could see the next marker. And we repeated that process. It was very slow. For some idiot reason the dogs trusted that I knew what I was doing.

We went fifteen miles in three hours. When it was getting dark there was absolutely no way to continue unless I wanted to do it as they did in the old days — with a compass. But when you're on sea ice and there could be open water, I didn't think it was a good idea. So I had to camp there for the night. That was an ordeal, getting settled in. It took me over two hours, I think, to get warm and halfway comfortable. My clothes had gotten damp and I had to switch into some dryer clothes inside my sled bag, which was an interesting process. It would have been hilarious to an onlooker.

It hadn't let up all night. My sled was rocking in the wind. The dogs were buried in snow the next morning. I could hardly see them. Getting started was tough, trying to get into boots and get organized without freezing my hands, doing zippers and so forth.

I was glad when I got to Koyuk. I was ready to kiss the snowbank.

It's a strange feeling coming into Nome. You've been out on

the trail so long at that point that you're operating in a strange state. You're used to doing this stuff all by yourself, isolated. You think you must look like someone from Mars. I couldn't believe it was happening. It took weeks to hit me that I'd won the Iditarod.

I was unprepared for the reaction. To have so many people pulling for you. Everybody from Northwest Alaska was so proud of me. I did it the hard way and that's what people were saying. And of course I had a lot of ladies pulling for me. There were so many good feelings. I was proud of my dogs. I never doubted them.

It's hard to imagine that winning it again would be as special as winning it in 1985.

I'm not one of those lifer types who run it every year. I would love to win the race again. Of course I would. I'd love to prove that these new dogs I have are good and I miss being out there on the trail.

"TAKING TURNS" (1984 print) expresses the cooperation among mushers who break trail for one another.

Rick Swenson, five-time Iditarod winner, became interested in dog mushing for travel into the wilderness of Minnesota, his home state.

CHAPTER 3:
RICK SWENSON

*R*ICK SWENSON, FORTY-ONE, is one of the stars of the Iditarod and one of the most recognizable faces in Alaska. He has a huge following and over the years has appeared on national TV to discuss the race.

Swenson raced in sixteen Iditarods and never has finished out of the top ten. That is the best overall record. He has won a record five times — in 1977, 1979, 1981, 1982, and again in 1991 in a storm-slowed race when he had to brave forbidding trail conditions after other competitors turned back. Swenson's famous leader in his early victories was a dog named Andy, for whom he later named his son.

Swenson lives and trains his dogs near Fairbanks. He is from Crane Lake, Minn., where he got his start in dog mushing.

I THINK THE KEY ELEMENT in what makes the Iditarod special is that it's in Alaska, which means it may rain, it may snow. In some sporting events, if it gets cloudy, they stop. The caution flag comes out. There have been proposals that if the weather gets too bad, the race should be stopped. That's not the Iditarod. Weather is part of the deal. If you think it's too bad for your own safety, then don't go.

When you have the attitude "I am having a good time" in storms, those situations aren't life-threatening or negative. They're positive. If you don't have that attitude, then things probably aren't going to work out for you. It doesn't matter if you're racing for first place or if you're just trying to get to the finish line. If you don't have that positive attitude, if you aren't enjoying trying to travel in those adverse conditions, then you're going to stop and crawl into a sleeping bag and wait for it to get better.

I got into dogs because I wanted to travel in the wilderness. That was when I was living up in the Boundary Waters Canoe Area, at Crane Lake, Minn., and that was the only way we could travel — either that or ski. If you wanted to go farther in a day than you could cross-country skiing, then you were going to have to step up to dogs.

Then I read about the first Iditarod and I said, "Gee, I'd sure like to do that some day." I was twenty-two. I moved to Alaska when I was twenty-three. I ran in the Iditarod in 1976. That was the dream, right? Just to run in the Iditarod. Just to get to Nome and get the belt buckle. Finish the Iditarod.

The first time it was an adventure. I had no illusions of winning that year, or ever winning. That was the only time I had any doubt as to whether I could get to Nome. Since then, I've never worried about that.

Unfortunately, because of all the sponsor pressure and media pressure, I don't have time anymore to meet those people who come for the adventure. It's not because I wouldn't like to, but running is such an intense thing now.

Any time you run in the race, whether you win or scratch, you should be able to say, "I can improve in this area and I can improve in that area." If you get to a point where you don't feel you can make any improvements, then you're going to be going downhill because there's somebody out there who's making improvements.

Just finishing gives anybody confidence. You've got twenty teams that should be in the top ten. The competition is close now. There's a personal satisfaction having won it, but back in the early days the Iditarod and sled-dog racing was different than it is now. None of us had sponsors. When I won in 1977 — I've got some pictures — I don't have a single patch on. I wasn't sponsored by anybody. I won $9,600 and that was it. I had to pay my way back from Nome.

In 1979, I think I had $2,000 worth of sponsors. The personal satisfaction of winning then, I think, was a bigger deal. You were doing it for your personal satisfaction. You weren't doing it because you were getting paid money and you had all these perks and opportunity if you could win.

The sled that I won the Iditarod with the first time, I built with hand tools, and I mean non-electric hand tools. Now people talk about a hand-made sled, they're using a table saw and power drills. I'm talking about hand tools.

It's a different era now. I bet half the people in the top twenty have never built a dogsled using power tools. I remember sewing harnesses. Joe Garnie is that kind of guy, every dog harness his dog wears, he still sews by hand. It's got the dog's name written on it. That guy has a tremendous wealth of knowledge of dogs.

I enjoy all the additional knowledge that I have now, but I'm nostalgic.

I could see from my first races that the event deserved attention. It deserves more attention than it's getting now. I would have never dreamed fifteen years ago that a disabled baseball player like this Bo whatever-his-name-is would be getting $100,000 a game to sit on the bench.

It's better these days for guys like me in many respects. But I still get the most satisfaction from people like Dick Wilmarth and Carl Huntington and the old champions. And when I go to

JEFF SCHULTZ

Rick Swenson pushes his sixteen-dog team through Dalzell Gorge between Rainy Pass and Rohn in the Alaska Range.

a Native village, to Huslia or someplace, and talk with Bobby Vent and Warner Vent, I get more satisfaction out of that and how those guys react to what I've done. Those are the people I held up as my idols when I started racing. George Attla was at my house and had coffee. I got more satisfaction sitting there talking with him about the 1991 race than I do talking with David Letterman.

It's as if you were a boxer and you could sit down at the table with Muhammad Ali and Sugar Ray Leonard and pretend you were fighting Roberto Duran and Mike Tyson — even if it's just b.s. We can sit there and talk about the great dogs we had.

I like the sound of "Rick Swenson, five-time winner of the Iditarod." I don't consider myself to be the greatest long-distance dog-musher who ever lived. I don't think any of us should consider ourselves that. I don't think we can hold a candle to some of the old-timers, guys like Leonhard Seppala.

Seppala and those guys stayed awake days on end just to train themselves for the All-Alaska Sweepstakes (in the early years of the twentieth century). Running miles and miles and miles all the time, hard, not just out there jogging for the fun of it. Running that All-Alaska Sweepstakes was a full-time, year-round job. They weren't out making publicity appearances. They were heroes in Nome.

I'd like to win it a few more times for my own personal satisfaction. But then I think it's essential for somebody new to break into the winner's circle. That would be good for the competitors' enthusiasm.

Each year when I go into the race, I don't worry about last year's race, or having won five times versus somebody who's won four. It's this year's race. Who's going to win this year? Last year is behind us, the storms, the moose attacks. We've all been through going the wrong way and having our dogs get sick and all these things. This is a new year. And who knows what's going to happen? But it'll be interesting. It'll be the Iditarod.

Susan Butcher makes good time on a stretch of Bering Sea ice near Elim.

Susan Butcher is a remarkable competitor who prefers looking ahead to new goals rather than reliving old glories.

CHAPTER 4:
SUSAN BUTCHER

*I*N 1985, SUSAN BUTCHER WAS the Iditarod favorite, but a moose attacked her team and knocked her out of the race. She came back the next year to win with a record-setting time of 11 days, 15 hours and 6 minutes flat, some seventeen hours faster than the old record. Butcher also won in 1987, 1988 and 1990, each time setting a record.

Over the years, Butcher has received many honors, including recognition from the Women's Sports Foundation as the Professional Athlete of the Year.

Probably the most famous Iditarod dog is Granite, who led Butcher's team to its first three victories, though as a pup Granite did not often show signs of becoming a great racing dog.

Butcher, thirty-seven, lives with her husband, Dave Monson, and more than one-hundred sled dogs in remote Eureka, about seventy-five air miles northeast of Fairbanks. Monson, who also has raced in the Iditarod, is a past champion of the Yukon Quest race between Fairbanks and Whitehorse, Yukon Territory, Canada.

Butcher grew up in Cambridge, Mass., and moved in the early 1970s to Colorado, where she began dog mushing. She moved to Alaska in 1975 and raced in her first Iditarod in 1978 after living alone in the wilderness in the Wrangell-St. Elias Range.

GRANITE IS A WONDERFUL DOG. Granite has so many faults I cannot see how that dog would have made it in somebody else's kennel. But he also has some incredible natural ability, and he has such a close relationship with me.

He has no confidence. As a puppy, he didn't even look like he'd make it as a sled dog, let alone as a lead dog. He was scared of his own shadow, scared of the other dogs. He didn't understand pulling, though he was naturally intelligent. I could throw him in lead and I might get one run every two weeks out of him. But then if you put him up there again he wouldn't even leave the dog yard. He wouldn't go.

He didn't have enough confidence. But then he had this strange combination of no confidence and a stubborn streak. So sometimes he'd become confident to do the wrong thing. Most people don't tolerate that with their sled dogs, but I let him go along for a while. A long while. He wasn't a fast trotter. Now, as it turned out, he had a beautiful fast trot, but he wouldn't show it to you. He was always loping, which a long-distance racer doesn't like to see in his dogs. But I liked him and I wanted to see him do well.

I offered Granite to David (before we were married) and he didn't want him. I tried to sell him, but nobody wanted him after I listed his faults.

He's got this cool personality. He had to work so hard to become a good dog, and I had to work so hard with him, that I think he's proud of what he's done. He's not a good leader at home during training runs, never has been, never has gotten to be one. He just learned to love racing.

It started to show when I took him as a team dog to the 1984 race. I've always had a kennel of one-hundred or so dogs, but most of them were puppies and yearlings and I had few team dogs. Literally any dog that was of the right age went into the team because someone would get injured. Granite wasn't making the team on his ability, but he made it because of his age.

That year, I made it across to Koyuk with Copilot in lead,

but somewhere, it must have been between Koyuk and Elim, I just didn't have any leaders. So Granite looked good.

He's just a pure mental athlete. He has good feet. But Granite doesn't eat. He'll eat one meal out of three. Makes you nervous, but he doesn't lose any weight. He eats and drinks when he needs to, and you have to have confidence that he's going to get himself fed.

In 1986, it was Granite's first year of being leader when I won. And he was a leader in 1987 when I won. The third win he was helpful. He made a big difference, but he wasn't the main leader. The next year I came in second to Joe Runyan and that year Granite wasn't much help, but I allowed him to cross the finish line in lead. He was on a sentimental journey in 1990. But he broke a toenail in Rohn, so I dropped him.

Granite was one of those neat dogs that everybody likes to have who will go up front at the beginning of the race and stay there because he loves it. He loves to be in lead in a race. What happened in 1988 is his best story.

In October of 1987 he became seriously ill. I rushed him to a vet in Fairbanks and we did the best we could for him and the vet basically said he was going to die. He had permanent heart, liver and kidney damage along with damage to his brain. I sat with him for forty-eight hours watching every breath and heartbeat. I mean, he was barely making it. He was a goner.

As best as we understand, it was a kidney infection that went undetected. He had no symptoms. And then he had heat stroke on top of it, caused by the infection, probably, because it wasn't even a hot day.

I pumped him full of fluids and we flew him down to Anchorage to Bob Sept at the Bering Sea Animal Clinic. I sat with him for two weeks and we brought him around.

Bob said that's fine, we've made him live, but he's never going to run again. I asked, "Not even with the pups?" He said no.

I knew Granite would be distraught not running. His test results were horrible. I brought him home and he was determined to get back on the team. I started taking him on puppy walks because I suppose I had this little hope. Bob wasn't even sure he was going to live long. He wasn't going to keel over tomorrow, but it didn't look good.

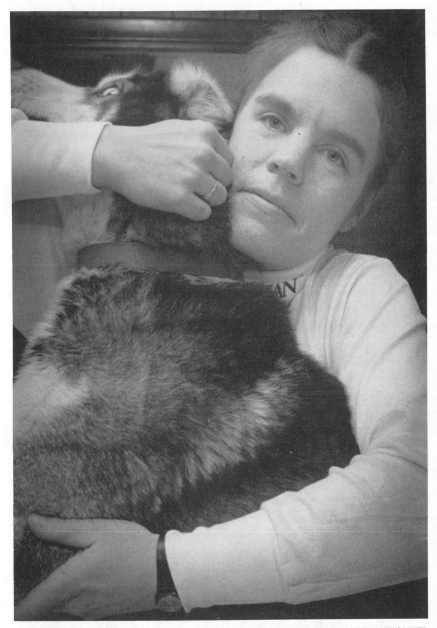

MIKE MATHERS/FAIRBANKS DAILY NEWS-MINER

Four–time winner Susan Butcher is known for the care and training she gives her dogs and for the loyalty they give her.

I took him on one-mile walks and I was testing his urine and blood twice a day. I hadn't given up. If he was to have any chance, I had to be on top of any changes in his system.

Later, Bob said go ahead and let him run the puppies. So I let him run the pups on two-mile runs. But to him it was punishment. He wanted to run with the team dogs and that's it. Every time the team dogs would go he'd be barking and jumping. Then I advanced him to the yearlings thinking he would like that better. He didn't want to go with the yearlings and he was so depressed.

Granite's tests were showing improvement, but not enough for us to feel confident. I was hooking up the dogs for a twenty-mile run when Granite had gone only ten miles that year. I put up the team dogs and he was going nuts. I thought to myself, "Well, who cares? I'll just let him run in the team because he wants to so badly. If I have to, I'll carry him home."

Well, as soon as we left the yard, and I had him in the lead, it started dumping snow. By the time we got to where we were ten miles from home, it was snowing hard and we were breaking trail through about six inches of snow.

So Granite was charging along, breaking trail, and by the time we got home, what should have been an hour-and-a-half run became a three-and-a-half-hour run.

So I ran him in the Portage 250 race in Unalakleet. I was happy with my team, with or without Granite, but I wanted him to get that third win.

In Unalakleet, I was down to two-year-olds who had never raced with Granite as their leader. My dogs were starting to tire and Rick Swenson's were feeling good, which is typical of a seasoned team. I could see him the whole time. I was timing him and he was two minutes behind me and finally caught up.

I thought, "That's it, I have tired two-year-olds." So I stopped and let Rick go by, and see, Granite is a racer, and I think he knows that we race against Rick. He knows who the competitive mushers are. He saw Rick go by and he just took off. He was literally towing those two-year-olds. Nobody was helping him pull and he was keeping up with Rick.

I stopped the team and made them sit until Granite got it out of his mind because I thought he was going to kill himself. I gave him about six minutes and off we went. Well, Rick was more tired than I knew and his dogs started faltering and Granite never stopped charging. We passed Rick and won it. So then I thought Granite was ready to run the Iditarod again.

The dogs have as much pride as any human athlete. That's why Granite's a wonderful dog. He knows when he's won. He thinks he deserves all the accolades, he expects them. He's a ham in front of the media.

When the Iditarod was organized in 1973 I knew I wanted to run it. I was a good musher and I'd been mushing for a lot of years, but I never liked racing because I'd only mushed sprint races. Although I like sprint racing now, I didn't like it then. My initial experience was in Colorado. I probably still wouldn't like sprint racing in Colorado.

I don't think my first Iditarod in 1978 was a wide-eyed experience. I'd lived in the Wrangell Mountains for so many years that I'd seen worse trail. I'd been more alone in the Bush with no one knowing where I was. The Iditarod is the biggest wilderness experience many mushers have had. It's the worst trail they've seen.

It was the funnest race. I had a great time. I met so many new friends and all the villagers. You gain confidence. I decided then that I wanted to win it.

I came to Alaska in 1975. My plan was to run the Iditarod for the experience, not for racing. I think after having trained for it, I already knew that I liked the competitive aspect. And after the first race I knew I could improve.

I always felt I was going to win the race. Your first win is in some ways your most exciting, but I feel my first race was the most exciting because everything was new. Nineteen-eighty-six was my ninth race, so there wasn't much new about the Iditarod Trail.

I felt confident in 1986. I felt confident in other years, too, and didn't win. It was a new team. My best team ever at that point was 1985. And most of the team had been obliterated by the moose. Only two were killed, but thirteen were injured. There were six veteran dogs out of sixteen in 1986. Not even all the veterans had raced with me.

I had written a plan. What I did was take my 1984 times — I ran a fabulous race in 1984, totally misjudged Dean Osmar, but ran a fabulous race — and I was planning to break the record. I thought, "Where can I take a chunk of time out?" Little bits of time, ten minutes here, twenty minutes there, and do it faster. When I added it up, it totaled eleven days, eleven hours — considerably under the record.

I thought, "I don't know if I can do it that fast." So I wrote a second, alternate plan that allowed more time, but it didn't seem to work for me. The first one worked. You were at the right places at daylight where you wanted to be at daylight, and you were at the right places at dark.

Most of the time when I win races, I'm not that excited. I'm happy but you haven't slept much and I think the joy is finishing. You almost don't realize for a day or two that you're actually done.

As soon as I'm in I don't like to talk about the race. I want to start talking about next year's race and what I plan to do. I set my goals the second I finish. That way, you don't have a letdown period. You're immediately working towards your next goal.

If I set the goal to win, then I expect to win.

"HER NAME WAS PIKAI" (1990 poster) honors the dog who led artist-musher Jon Van Zyle to Nome in 1976 and 1979.

Rick Mackey got his start as a youngster running in three-dog sprint races in Anchorage. At eighteen, he competed in the world championship.

CHAPTER 5:
RICK MACKEY

*R*ICK MACKEY, THIRTY-EIGHT, has been racing sled dogs as long as he can remember. His first competition as a youngster was in three-dog sprint races at the Tudor Track in Anchorage.

At eighteen, he raced in the Anchorage Fur Rendezvous World Championship, but decided that long-distance mushing might be more his style when he realized it would take years to put together a team capable of challenging world-champion sprinter George Attla.

Following his father's lead, Rick switched to long-distance racing and made his debut in the Iditarod in 1975 at age twenty-one.

Mackey, winner of the 1983 race, has raced in the Iditarod fourteen times. He and his father, Dick, champion of the 1978 race, are the only father-son winners.

Mackey lives with his family in the Tanana River town of Nenana fifty-three miles south of Fairbanks.

*I*N 1983, THE YEAR I WON, I had a good training year. We were living in Wasilla and I started training there the first part of November of 1982. I got into a big hassle with my neighbor and he got a petition going. They were complaining about my dogs barking all the time.

Every time I'd hook up a team the dogs would start raising heck and the neighbor was out there emptying a five-shot shotgun to shut them up. Of course, that scared the heck out of my dogs.

My family saw that we had to get out of Wasilla. We knew Dewey Halverson and Bobby Lee and some of the guys from Trapper Creek, so we went up there and they helped us find a place. It was a small sixteen-by-sixteen cabin and we camped out in it and trained dogs, me and my wife Patty and daughter Brenda, who was five or six, and my brother Bill, who was a handler.

We were there four months. No distractions. We didn't even go check our mail. We were having it collected in Wasilla. We had a good-sized house with running water and everything back in Wasilla and here we were melting snow for sixty dogs. Melting snow and burning nothing but wood and living in a shack was what it amounted to. It had Visqueen on the windows, no conveniences whatsoever. I had more miles on the dogs than I've ever had in all fourteen races.

When we left Fourth Avenue in 1983 it was zoom! The team got stronger and stronger. It was almost like I couldn't make a mistake. The coldest it got was probably twenty-five below. There weren't any major storms, just a little wind here and there — normal stuff. There was one spot on the Yukon River where we got held up. Larry "Cowboy" Smith and Eep Anderson got through and it was blowing like heck. You couldn't see the trail at all.

Dewey Halverson and Susan Butcher and I were together, and them danged dogs didn't want to go through there for nothing. You couldn't move. Anyway, ol' Herbie Nayokpuk

JEFF SCHULTZ

Rick Mackey, his clothing covered with sponsors' patches, runs his team on the trail between Kaltag and Unalakleet.

comes up like the Lone Ranger, just loping up. This is his territory. He's from Shishmaref. Dewey and I, we sic Susan on him: "Go see if you can talk Herbie into going first." Herbie, he doesn't like to go first, even though he has capable dogs.

So, Susan goes over: "Well, Herbie, how are you doing? We can't go, it's too windy. Our leaders won't go, you think you can go?" He says, "Well, I don't know, young leaders, young leaders, I'll try." He takes off and charges right through. It was hard-packed snow, but it was blowing so hard.

I got to Kaltag, and Eep and Cowboy were the leaders. They had about four hours on me, Susan, Dewey and Herbie. We needed to rest and they were going to be about six hours ahead of us when it was time to go. Right there I figured I could beat everybody in the group, if nobody caught up with us.

My team was still in good shape and eating well. I got over to Shaktoolik and now Cowboy was only two hours in front. Eep was holding his own. I'd only gained about an hour on him between Kaltag and Shaktoolik. He was about five hours in front.

It was calm and clear. Ten to twenty below. Light snow cover, decent trail, no problem finding it. I got to Shaktoolik and heard Cowboy had left two hours before. Cowboy was moving slow. I caught him twenty miles out. He was walking. He was all done. Now it was a matter of getting Eep. I'm second now. There's only one guy ahead of me.

Here it is noon and Eep's rested five hours. This is leaving Koyuk. I'd just run straight across from Shaktoolik to Koyuk so I gotta rest. It's hot as heck, sun beating down and Eep, there he goes. My dogs aren't eating, and here Eep goes, and Cowboy comes in and he's getting ready to take right off. And I'm going, "Heck, I gotta get going."

Herbie didn't want to go because it was too sunny — he doesn't like to run his dogs in the heat. But he left, too, and now three of them have left. And I still got my stuff scattered around. I drop a dog. It's a panic situation. I pulled into Koyuk second, and all of a sudden there's three guys gone and this is just an hour later. I'm all disorganized.

I threw all my stuff together and I took off. I caught Herbie and Cowboy after a couple hours. I didn't see Eep. I gained an hour on him into Elim. Four hours behind. I stayed there just one hour then took off for White Mountain.

I knew I was going faster, but I didn't know if there was enough time to catch him.

At White Mountain, I'm two hours behind. I watched Eep leave. You could tell his dogs didn't want to go. They're tired. Still, two hours is a lot of time to gain on somebody unless they're walking.

I got to Topkok and I hadn't seen him. Here we are, halfway to Nome and I haven't even seen a glimpse of anything in front of me. Nothing is moving. And I was going pretty good. I was right down to my wool shirt, just pumping for all I was worth.

It's about forty miles to the top of Topkok. You're up a series of hills. No runner tracks. It was like he wasn't even in front of me. If you start seeing something, it'll give you a little encouragement to push harder. I kept going and wondering and looking.

Finally, there was a trailbreaker. I flagged him down. "Seen Eep up there?" He said, "Yeah, he's about ten miles in front of you." It sounded like I had an hour of the two hours back. It was looking like it was going to be awful close. Thirty-seven miles to go and I've still got to get another hour. But at least I'm going.

I'm hyped now. I'm one hour behind from winning the goddamn Iditarod. I mean, man, I'm going, but I'm tired as heck. The last time I slept was in Unalakleet and that was forty-five minutes. Hadn't slept a wink since. I was wasted, let me tell you. And the sun was setting behind Nome, so it was a sleepy time of day as I hit the coast. You're staring right into the sun. I dozed off.

The sun finally went away and I was all right. I pulled into Safety at dark and Eep was only ten minutes in front.

That was when I knew I could do it. I switched lead dogs around. I dropped this one two-year-old and, man, I took off like a wild man. I probably caught him in the first couple miles. I had my light off. He did too. Just as I was catching him I saw the outline of his back. My leaders were probably fifty feet from him. "Wow," I thought, "there he is!" I about ran into the back of his legs.

He looked back over his right shoulder and then I told my

dogs to go on by and they just kept a-movin'. We didn't say anything to each other. I could look back and see the dog team. I could even hear him. I knew he was driving them. I'm afraid my dogs are going to miss the trail. They're running in the dark, too, that first darkness of evening. There's no moon or stars or anything. By now we're getting near Cape Nome and you have to wind through some icebergs and chunks. I've been goofed up there before.

"QUIETLY, UNNOTICED, I TOUCHED THE PAST" (1979 poster) reflects the rich history of the Iditarod Trail.

By now we've only got twelve miles to go. But then we hit soft snow, about a foot deep. It was corn snow going around the Cape. I had this big wheel dog that started wobbling around in it. I had to slow down to get him through the soft stuff. And then I could hear Eep back there. Couldn't see him. But you can hear a musher's voice when it's quiet. You can see all the lights of Nome by now and it's starting to get brighter.

I rested the wheel dog through there for about twenty minutes, three or four miles, and started thinking, "Heck, I better get moving." This old dog got better. Once he saw the lights of Nome he came on like a freight train.

People were all over the place at Howard Farley's Fish Camp. Now we're about five miles from the end.

As I came up onto Front Street — you come off the ice there — I was amazed how much my dogs had left. The absolute strongest team I had ever run. At the same time it's going through my head as I'm comin' down the street, "You're the first one getting under this arch. Ain't that something?"

My wife Patty and my dad were at the finish line. We were darned happy. We opened a bottle of champagne right then, but I was tired. Early the next morning, everybody was up, and I sat up in bed. I didn't know what the heck it was exactly I was yelling, but it was something like, "Where's Eep. What time did he leave?" I had slept ten hours and woke up in a sweat. I was still racing Eep.

Then it started sinking in — my dad winning too, being the only father and son team.

When they're looking in the history books years from now my grandkids will say, "Yeah, that must have been a tough breed, them Mackeys. They had two of them that won it." That's what makes it special.

I started training the next year to go back and win again. And that's what it's been every year since then. I want to win the race at least one more time. If I were to get lucky and win it this year I'm sure I'd go for a third win. If it takes me until I'm fifty or sixty to win it a second time, I think I'll call that good enough.

I don't doubt that I will win it again. I flat believe it. I'm going to win the son of a gun.

"DALZELL MEMORIES" *(from a 1991 poster) portrays one of the many hazards found on the Iditarod Trail.*

Martin Buser began dog mushing in Switzerland, then moved to Alaska where he ran the Iditarod in 1980 and climbed Mt. McKinley a year later.

JEFF SCHULTZ

CHAPTER 6:
MARTIN BUSER

*I*N 1991, MARTIN BUSER CHASED Rick Swenson for seventy-seven miles through howling wind, frigid temperatures and blizzard conditions from White Mountain into Nome, venturing into a dangerous storm that forced three other top mushers to turn back.

Swenson finished first, Buser second. It was an unforgettable experience that formed a bond between the two men.

Buser, thirty-three, lives at Big Lake near Anchorage with his wife Kathy, an elementary-school teacher, and their two young sons, Rohn and Nikolai, who are named after Iditarod checkpoints. Buser won the 1992 race.

Buser is from Switzerland, where he discovered dog mushing. He has been in Alaska since 1980 when he first ran the Iditarod. A year later, he climbed Mount McKinley, at 20,320 feet the highest peak in North America.

*I*N 1991, I WAS THE LAST ONE to leave White Mountain behind Susan Butcher, Joe Runyan, Tim Osmar and Rick Swenson. I think it was four in the morning. It was snowing and blowing.

I knew it was going to storm. It always storms when I'm there. That's a given. "If you guys don't want a storm," I tell everybody, "just don't let me race." Earlier, I got to Unalakleet under blue skies and said, "Where's my storm? It's coming. Wait a few hours." I went into the house of my host family, had a nice dinner, came back out and the storm was roaring. It was unreal.

So it was tough going after I had gone a couple hours from White Mountain. It seemed like I kept getting turned around and it was dark, and there were no reflectors. Visibility was probably a dog-team length, fifty or sixty feet. It was not bad yet. But it was windy, strong winds. At one point a snowmachine came by going toward Safety, and I benefited from that snowmachine for about five minutes. I tried to follow its trail and couldn't. It was a fresh trail and when it's blowing like that you can't find it. An old trail you can, if it's set up before the storm set in. You can find ripples in the snow. I call them railroad tracks.

And then a team comes toward me! It was Susan. I said, "Hey, you're going the wrong way, girl." She said, "Well, it depends on who you talk to." And she proceeded to tell me how she had to help Swenson with his gloves, he had frozen hands, he had problems with his headlamp, she had to help him out, and he wasn't doing too well out there. It couldn't be done, Martin, she said. She was going to turn around and go back to White Mountain.

We talked two minutes at the most. Those storms are noisy. And I told her, "Well, I'll go find out for myself." I wasn't about to turn around unless I was sure everybody turned around. So I took off and a couple minutes later I had a head-on with Osmar. Another minute later, I had a head-on with Runyan. I didn't talk to those two teams. I waved.

There was still one team out. I could count. I was well-

An Iditarod musher and team look small from the air on a frozen river bottom.

prepared with equipment and food for myself and the dogs. I had the best clothing available. When I left I knew this might take forty-eight hours from White Mountain.

Normally, it's eight, eight and a half, maybe. I was trying to envision the worst-case scenario. Having a loaded sled slowed me down, but it also made it possible for me to go through.

Knowing Rick was still out there, I wasn't about to turn around. Well, come to find out Rick didn't know anyone had turned around. He had no idea. I think the first time Rick found out was at the shelter cabin on the other side of Topkok.

Then it got worse. Occasionally, we'd go by stakes, trail markers. I figured I would never let myself go a hundred yards without being sure I was on the trail. You can get lost so easily. It was hard-packed, so the dogs tend to want to go with the wind. They don't want to buck that wind. We kept doughnutting around looking for the trail.

It finally became clear that I needed to lead. They could not see. I call myself the guy with the sled. Throughout the whole race I'm a burden to those dogs. In the dogs' point of view, "Us four-legged animals, we're so far superior, we can go five times as fast as the guy with the sled." I went up to Eleanor, my key leader, and I told her, "We'll work this out together."

I put her in a single lead. I grabbed one of the tug lines and together we started looking for those little ripples that the snowmachines make. Often, just between my feet was the only spot I could see them.

I was pulling on the tug line. One hand, head down, Eleanor was right next to me. It was cold, but I was sheltered. Really good gear. I call it my cocoon. I was dressed for the occasion. I was not cold. Throughout the race, I was never cold, other than my face. That's the problem. I had a lot of my face exposed. Every year I get what I call my Norton Sound Facelift. I get a new layer of skin. Instead of getting older, I get younger every time I race. Two weeks after the race, I got a layer of baby skin on my face, courtesy of the Iditarod Trail Committee with no extra charge.

It was slow progress. The guy with the sled, under those conditions, makes maybe three-and-a-half, four miles per hour at the most. At one point, we got off the trail and we couldn't find it.

That was midday. I said, "Break time," huddled everybody together. We got in a bunch. I do a lot of huddling. My dogs, they like to sniff each other, socialize. They're just a happy-go-lucky bunch of dogs getting together. By doing that they benefit from each other's body warmth. I pile 'em up as close as they want to each other. There was nothing to do but wait. I didn't want to wander around. I didn't want to leave my dogs.

I know Rick is out there somewhere. I could be fifty yards from him. I could never hear him, nor would I see him. I was minding my own business, making headway if I could.

I knew where he was when I got to the shelter cabin at the bottom of Topkok. There was a stranded snowmachiner there. He had a fire going. He was out collecting firewood as I was coming off the hill and had it all warm because he had been there a day and a half already. Of course, Rick had asked him to be as vague as possible, but Rick had also written on the wall that he had the race won by then. Pretty confident. He had left an hour and a half before I got there.

That was the first time I could relax enough to rig up my Walkman and start tuning in to the radio. I heard that nobody knew where I was. That was funny because I knew all along where I was. There are two things that make people tick. One is knowing who you are and the other is knowing where you are. It's true that if you take one of the two away — and usually it's knowing where you are — people get nervous, to the point where they get frightened or uncomfortable or uneasy. And some of them go nuts. I know who I am.

I was chasing Rick and had the feeling that I was making progress. That last twenty-four hours of the race were taxing. They took the utmost concentration. On top of accumulated lack of sleep, you've got to make the right decisions continuously.

After Topkok, I went into what I call my Stealth mode. I kept on my white wind garment. By now the conditions were improving. Visibility was better.

One of my hopes was for Rick to relax too much in Safety and fall asleep, maybe stay a little longer than he had planned. Everybody was sleeping in Safety. But Rick had left. I stopped for about a minute and a half. Speedwise, there was no reason to push the dogs and hope to catch him. That was mathematically impossible, a remote chance.

In Nome, people came up to say, "Man, we were worried where you were."

The unspoken bond that Rick and I felt, after that storm — unspoken, mind you — is strong. There were handshakes and hugs between us and they said as much as words. Not much needs to be said. We both did it and it was the same for both of us.

Only people who have had that experience can feel the bond.

A scene from the 1991 poster, "CAMPFIRE CAMARADERIE."

Norman Vaughan began racing the Iditarod when most men his age were slowing down.

CHAPTER 7:

NORMAN VAUGHAN

*N*ORMAN VAUGHAN, EIGHTY-FIVE, of Anchorage, has mushed dogs for nearly seventy years. His life has been one adventure after another. When he was in his twenties, living north of Boston in Hamilton, Mass., he joined Admiral Richard Byrd's famed expeditions to Antarctica.

During World War II, Vaughan attained the rank of colonel and led a dramatic sled-dog rescue of flyers downed in Greenland. Decades later, as an octogenarian, he spent several summers participating in the search and discovery of the downed planes.

Vaughan worked as a handler with famed sprint musher Dr. Roland Lombard of Wayland, Mass., a many-time world and North American champion. He met his wife, Carolyn Muegge-Vaughan, through dog mushing and has become a hero to senior citizens.

Vaughan completed the 1990 Iditarod in 21 days, 10 hours, 26 minutes, 26 seconds at age eighty-three after hardships forced him out of earlier races.

In the summer of 1991, Vaughan was elected to the Mushers Hall of Fame. The plaque read, in part: "His beautiful expression of a desire for the best from himself and on every trail inspires all who come in contact with him — the young and the young at heart."

*M*Y FIRST EXPOSURE TO SLED DOGS was in 1917 when I was twelve. My friend Edward Goodale, who lived less than five miles away in Massachusetts, and I both read a couple of Arctic books of the real explorers. We were excited that they traveled by dog team. We said, "Why don't we see if we can harness our fathers' dogs?" His father had a German shepherd and my father had a collie.

We made rope harnesses like the natives on the east coast of Labrador and Newfoundland originally did. Put our dogs in harness and when we said "Mush!" the dogs turned around and got up on the sled, wagging their tails and wanting to be petted.

One of us became the leader, and the dogs followed and pulled us on an old Flexible Flyer sled. Very poor sledding. The snow wasn't good. We got a kick out of being pulled by a dog and we bought dogs at the pound for ten dollars. They only had one eye and things like that, but we had a team.

I left Harvard University a few years later because I had spent too much time in football and my marks weren't up. I would go on probation. If I went away for the winter and had a good record, I could come back in full standing in the fall. I said, "Great, I'll do that." I went to Dr. Wilfred Grenfell's on the Labrador coast, which, in the wintertime, was heaven for me because to get there was a three-hundred-mile trip by dog team. I never had been on a big team before. So I went there and learned to drive dogs. That was in the winter of 1925.

During World War II, I was involved in the rescue by dog team of these planes in Greenland. We rescued twenty-five men, which was the entire air crew of those eight airplanes, and not one of them died. There was no other way of doing it. There were no helicopters in those days and no plane we could find that had skis.

I first came to Alaska in 1952. I was in the service at the Pentagon and asked if I could go to Alaska on a space-available basis. I wanted to compete in the North American Sled Dog Championships in Fairbanks. I came in tenth. Horace "Holy"

Smoke was the winner. I kept coming up between 1952 and 1974 when I came for good. I worked with Dr. Roland Lombard as his handler when he was winning his world championships. I raced the second team for Dr. Lombard down in Kenai and in other places. Dr. Lombard, as anybody knew, was a great man who did more for dog driving in Alaska than he's been given credit for.

I came up in 1974 in time to hear about the Iditarod. I immediately got a snowmachine and went out into the Knik area, brushing down the trail as a volunteer. My reaction was, "I've got to get in this!" I knew only the best drivers in the world would be able to do a thousand miles. And I wanted to be one of them.

The 1990 Iditarod was my most satisfying. I was 83 and crazy to do it.

The team took off down Fourth Avenue. I heard one yell as I went along: "All the way! All the way!" They were wishing me luck to go all the way to Nome. Of course, they knew how damned old I was.

They cared about me because they knew I didn't have any money and had to work hard to get sponsors. They knew I'd tried before and failed and kept trying. They also knew that in two races before I had to scratch — one because I froze both feet and the other because I got lost.

All the way. That was my motto.

I got into the middle of the race and there was one place where there was a bank and we went off the top, down ten or fifteen feet. It knocked me out for a minute. I was dizzy.

One night was really cold. I was traveling with Steve Haver. We decided we'd better stop, it was so damn cold. I remember I couldn't get in my bag. I was shivering, trying to stay warm. I got into my bag halfway and I couldn't get it up over my shoulders. All my parkas were on but I was still cold. So we finally yelled to each other, "Let's go on." We had forty miles to go before we got somewhere and that was six hours or so.

I fell into the water the next to last day, on some ice between White Mountain and Safety. Steve Haver was ahead of me. He went across the ice. I thought it was safe. My dogs went across after him and all of a sudden the ice broke on one side of the sled.

We were going so slowly that I didn't lose the team, but here

I was on my side in a foot-and-a-half, two feet of water.

You don't get wet until you stand up, and then the water has seeped through and you begin to feel wet, and then it's cold. Steve said, "Hell, you've got to change your clothes right now or you'll freeze up." He was right, of course, even though only half of me was soaking wet.

The challenge for me isn't to win. The challenge is to get to Nome. I broke six ribs on one trip, in 1986. I was thrown off the sled when it tipped sideways going across frozen tussocks just before the Farewell Burn area. I was rescued by helicopter.

The Iditarod is the greatest prolonged challenge you can undertake voluntarily. It's great. When the weather is fine, you think you've died and gone to heaven. The people are tremendous in the villages. That's when you begin to realize what a nice world this is to live in. When they greet you and say, "Put your

NORA GRUNER/FAIRBANKS DAILY NEWS-MINER

Norman Vaughan signs copies of "With Byrd at the Bottom of the World," his book about adventures in Antarctica.

dogs up here and come into my home."

The disadvantage of my age is that I'm stiff and slow. I'd like to run when I can't. I'd like to run up to my dogs and I can't do that. While the dogs are going, if they're only walking, I can't run up faster than my dogs and fix a harness, fix a line and let the sled come by me and jump on. I've had a bad leg and now I've got a brand-new knee from surgery. But you can't get frustrated.

I was less patient when I was younger. I had to have everything done that minute. I was jumping and running all the time to get something done. Now I just walk.

The advantage of my age is the support from the people and other dog drivers. If I dropped a glove or a piece of clothing, not only would a musher pick it up, but they'd stop and bring it up. When I broke my sled another time out on the Burn and couldn't go because there weren't any handlebars, one fellow came along and said, "Look, you need to finish this race. You take my sled and I'll take yours." He was serious about this. Maybe he thought it was a good idea to have an old man get to Nome.

I get that support all the time. People speak to you on the street. They don't think an old guy's going to win, but they get tired of reading only about Susan Butcher and Rick Swenson. So they look for other things to make it a complete race.

Without the rookies — and I travel more with the rookies — there wouldn't be much of a race. If you cut this race down to thirty people and built the prize to $100,000, it would be a great sensation for a week. But if you cut it down to just the fast teams, you would have only teams backed by big companies. It would lose a lot.

The Iditarod should be open to everybody. It's an Alaskan race. It's not a race for the champions.

Race Veteran Joe Redington often loans or leases sled dog teams to beginners.

JEFF SCHULTZ

Joe Redington was given a husky puppy when he arrived in Alaska to start a new home after World War II. Now he has nearly five-hundred dogs.

CHAPTER 8:
JOE REDINGTON

*J*OE REDINGTON, SEVENTY-FIVE, is called the Father of the Iditarod for his role as a founder of the race in 1973. He believed the race would revive dormant interest in sled dogs in Alaska. The first year, he organized the mushers and almost single-handedly raised the $50,000 purse for prizes.

Redington also is credited with reviving interest in the historic Iditarod Trail, where Leonhard Seppala mushed from Nenana to Nome in 1925 carrying medicine to treat an outbreak of diphtheria.

Over the years, Redington has run in all but one Iditarod — the first one. His best finish was fifth, but he still hopes to win some day.

Redington lives in Knik near Anchorage with his wife Vi. A native of Oklahoma who grew up about twenty-five miles from Philadelphia, Redington drove to Alaska after World War II to establish a new home. Just as he and Vi crossed the border from Canada, they were given a husky pup. That was the origin of the largest dog lot in Alaska.

Now, the Redingtons have between four- and five-hundred dogs and every year Joe leases several teams to beginners who wish to try their luck on the Iditarod Trail.

I HAVE TO ADMIT that I didn't think the Iditarod ever would get as big as it has. The Iditarod is known everywhere.

The recognition came in 1985 when Libby Riddles became the first woman to win. The word got out. Everybody knew it was one of the toughest races in the world.

Here was a sport that's the toughest there is and here's a woman who goes in there and tells them she's better than they are.

In 1973, the first year, we didn't know if we could get to Nome and we didn't have a dime for the $50,000 prize money I had promised.

I went to the banks and they turned me down cold. Some of them said, "Joe, you're crazy, butting your head against something like that. You don't even know if anybody will get to Nome." I said, "Well, they used to get there, why can't we get there again?"

It's something the public wanted at that time because sprint racing was dying. You couldn't find one person in fifty who knew anything about the Iditarod Trail. It had been dead so long.

When we got to Nome that year, we had our banquet in a bar. I asked, "Would you like to see another race?" And everybody shouted, "Yes!" I said, "OK, we'll put you on a bigger and better one next year." And we have been able to do that every year.

In 1991, I had seven teams in the race. I encourage people to lease teams. Sometimes they get a team for nothing. Sometimes they have to pay for it. We had two Russians, one Japanese musher and two from England. So it is a worldwide event. In 1978, I had one of the first foreign mushers, from Australia. And then I had one from Norway.

When we started the race, dogs were disappearing. We have more dogs in Alaska now than we ever had. And due to all the publicity, we were able to get the Iditarod Trail into the national trail system.

The most interesting time I had was when I led the field in 1988 for a little over half the race. I'm the only musher that's done the halfway mark in less than five days. That was to Cripple. I won $2,000 worth of silver coins.

The dogs were perfect. They were enjoying it and we went from one checkpoint to another and caught musher after musher until we were out front.

In Cripple, the four snowmachines that break trail were sitting in front of me and I couldn't find the drivers. The trail hadn't been broken. They said, "We didn't expect you until tomorrow."

I got a little peeved. They'd been there nine hours and I don't feel that I got a fair shake. I said to the drivers, "Let's get going." They said, "We want to get some coffee first." I said, "You've been sitting here for nine hours."

They got angry and jumped on their machines and went out of there wide open and tore up what little trail there was. The snow was right up to my dogs' bellies. I turned back. And I waited. I was there nine hours and still managed to get to Ruby, the first one to the Yukon River.

I felt there was a good chance of winning it. When I got to Kaltag I rested the dogs four hours and they were eager to go. Susan Butcher got there next. I left four hours ahead of her and went out about fifteen miles.

It was snowing hard. I couldn't find the trail. I found some snowmachiners who were camped. They couldn't find the trail either. I looked for the trail for about an hour and gave up.

So I went in and fell asleep in the little tent they had. When I woke up, Susan was in there asleep, too.

It was snowing and blowing and hard to find the trail. From then on I dropped but I managed to place fifth, which satisfied me. I don't have to win to have fun.

I'll be seventy-five for the 1992 race. You're not as good when you get older, but you can help yourself. I'm lifting weights and I've made some long swims. And as you get older, you get a little smarter.

If I'm gonna win it, I better do something pretty soon, you know?

"IN DISCOVERY OF SELF" (1988 poster) *symbolizes a musher's self discovery on the long trail to Nome.*

"Dewey" Halverson finished second in 1985 and says "that was the worst year you could have finished second — behind the first woman to win it."

CHAPTER 9:
DEWEY HALVERSON

*D*UANE "DEWEY" HALVERSON MAKES JOKES about having the misfortune of placing second in 1985 when Libby Riddles became the first woman to win. That was the stormy year the race was "frozen" — halted temporarily — by race officials because of problems distributing food and supplies along the trail.

Halverson, thirty-nine, operates a sled-dog racing exhibit and gift shop near Denali National Park during the summer and guides grizzly-bear hunters in the fall. He guides with fellow musher Jerry Austin and some years the two veterans plot their strategy as they sit around the campfire taking a break from the hunt.

Halverson lives in Anchorge. He has competed in seven Iditarods and his wife, Kathy, has run once. The couple has a young daughter.

THE 1985 RACE IS WHEN I shot the moose that knocked Susan Butcher's team out of the race. It was in that hilly, twisty area around Rabbit Lake and it's a hazard in there for moose. Your dog team's on the moose before you have an idea the thing's there. I came up and I could see a headlamp in front of me and I could hear, "Oh, hey, whoa!"

So I stop and ask, "What's going on?" And it's Susan saying, "There was a moose in my team, have you got a gun?" Well, she didn't have a gun. It was too much weight to carry. That killed me. Everybody felt sorry for her, but it's like running the Iditarod without your parka or harnesses. Whose fault is it, really? I don't feel there's much excuse for it. It wasn't an act of God that she couldn't finish the race that year.

I had a gun, a little .44-caliber Bulldog. It's almost like a Saturday Night Special. It's got a short barrel and it's a light-weight pistol, yet you can pack enough punch to kill a moose.

The dogs were trying to make themselves disappear into the snow. It was dead quiet and there's this big cow moose standing right in the middle of the team. I walked up there and shot twice. The moose had her head down. I must have hit her because she turned around and started up the trail, went up to the front of the team and started kicking more dogs. Then you could hear dogs screaming.

I was waiting to get another shot. There were a couple of trees alongside the trail. Pretty soon she turned around, put her head down and started coming right to the sled after us. I knew it was warfare by that time. I had three more bullets and no extras, so I shot two more times and finally, on the third shot, she stopped. She just stood there and all of a sudden I could see her wobble. Then over she went. Boom.

I felt sorry for Susan. I put my arms around her and gave her a hug. I said, "Take care of your dogs, take care of business. I'm going to feed mine, snack my dogs." It was like, "Let's not let this trauma take over everything else." I was sympathetic to her, to what was happening. I was sympathetic to this dead moose over there, too, but I wasn't about to do anything until I parked my dogs decently and fed them and made sure that I utilized the time that I was standing still.

By that time another couple of teams had come up. Jerry Austin helped me. We gutted the moose with our ax, just literally blew the whole rib cage out to get the job done as fast as we could because legally I had to gut it. I wanted to leave the moose in the middle of the trail as a novelty item for people to run over in the middle of the night. They said, "No, no." So we pulled it off the trail.

Another version of that story I tell tourists was that I came up, saw this massive bulk on the trail, unloaded my pistol and damn, I missed Susan and hit the moose! Everybody was pissed off at me about that.

When we pulled into Shaktoolik, I was second or third. John Cooper, who lived in Ambler then, but now lives in Thailand, was right in there. Libby Riddles was out two hours and camped all night. I wasn't concerned at that point.

I knew she couldn't go anywhere. Where we made a mistake was not knowing the country in Koyuk, the way the weather traditionally goes. The winds kind of die down in midday and then pick up again in the evening. That's what I've been told.

Cooper and I got up before daybreak the next morning and I got a weather report. They said the winds were going to abate around noon in Shaktoolik. So we just sat down and figured out on our watches and said, "Maybe the best time to leave here, instead of driving the snot out of the dogs in the team, is to leave here around ten o'clock, eleven o'clock in the morning. That will give us time to catch Libby and we can get through there." And I think that plan would have worked, too, because we talked to the ABC-TV crew out on the ice when they stopped to film us. We were only twenty miles out of Koyuk and Libby had just gotten into Koyuk. So, essentially, she was only two and a half hours ahead of us.

Unfortunately, the weather shut us down, plus the trail markers were nonexistent going into Koyuk. To go that last twenty miles took six hours. We finally got to a point where Cooper would park the team, I'd drive my team up ahead, park it, then I'd walk out ahead. When I found markers or trail, I'd signal him. We'd leapfrog that way. It was a whiteout. Any exposed flesh was frostbitten. Blowing right in your face. Ground blizzard. Boy, I had a heck of a leader that year, though. That dog Misty was incredible.

Cooper and I stopped and shared snacks behind the sled. I came up to him and said, "God, isn't this a great adventure?" I was laughing about it. The wind was blowing crap all over, we were hunkered down and he looked at me like I was out of my mind.

We were able to get into Koyuk and found out that Libby was seven hours ahead. I didn't give up. I thought she might make a wrong turn or something. I whittled it down to only the two hours she won by, but still, it was a day late and a dollar short.

And that was the worst year you could have finished second — behind the first woman to win it.

One year we were in Nome and there was a group of people sitting around a living room and they asked me why I hadn't run that year. I said, "Sponsorships." They said, "Well, you've got a good race record." I said, "I'm not a champion yet." I did have a good race record, but I didn't have that word "champion" with my name. I said, "Second doesn't cut it."

They argued with me. I said, "All right, who was second in 1985?" Boy, everybody sat around and scratched their heads. "Was that the year Libby won?" Nobody could figure it out. I said, "Well, I'm not sure, but I think it was me." Everybody turned red-faced. I said, "OK, is the point made here or not?"

The 1988 race was a disaster for me and I was twenty-seventh. We had trained in Ambler all winter. It was fifty below consistently, I mean for three weeks at a shot.

We came to Anchorage about two weeks before the race and I felt at the start that the dogs were acclimated to the weather. I was confident, but I came into Finger Lake with four dogs in the basket. It was 48 above that day! You're talking about a one-hundred-degree difference.

I've never been one for scratching. I don't believe in it. I think it takes something away from the race if you're going to pick up your ball and go home. It says something to stick it out. I lived most top drivers' worst nightmares — that their team falls apart.

The problem rests on my shoulders, not anybody else's. It's not bad dogs. It wasn't even the weather. It was me. I knew traditionally it was going to be warmer down there.

I had six dogs from Galena. That was the extent of my dog team and I had five out of Unalakleet and yet kept up with this pack of people who had bigger, faster teams. One of them was goading me at White Mountain. He said, "Well, here's Dewey with his little five-dog team, just plodding along." We were eating dinner, and I looked up at him and said, "Yeah, but we're still eating dinner together." Like, you figure it out, buddy, who's doing bad here, you or me?

I remember pulling into Nome that year, one of my worst finishes but my most memorable. All my peers were at the finish line. And not necessarily because everybody is wild about me. They were there taking note of my tenacity in finishing. Susan and Rick were within rock-throwing distance of one another. Joe Redington was there. Bill Cotter. Jerry Austin had a gin and tonic for me.

It touched my heart to have those people there.

"TODAY'S DREAMS, TOMORROW'S TRAIL, YESTERDAY'S MEMORIES" (1981 poster) imagines Iditarod racers of the future.

JEFF SCHULTZ

Rookie Kathy Halverson, an Anchorage school teacher, played a supporting role in one of the Iditarod's most dramatic episodes in 1989.

CHAPTER 10:
KATHY HALVERSON

*K*ATHY HALVERSON, THIRTY-TWO, raced the Iditarod just once, in 1989, but played an important role in one of the most dramatic episodes in Iditarod history.

Halverson and several other mostly rookie mushers gave up a chance to finish in the top twenty money and earn rookie-of-the-year honors to rescue North Pole, Alaska, musher Mike Madden.

Madden had collapsed on a remote portion of the trail between Ophir and Iditarod, suffering from what later was diagnosed as salmonella poisoning. Madden was cared for and nurtured by the small group of mushers until help arrived. Kathy Halverson and the other good samaritans were given a special award recognizing their selflessness on the trail.

Halverson was introduced to sled-dog racing by her husband, Dewey. She traveled the trail observing mushers and soaking up their expertise for several years before deciding to give it a try.

*I*WAS NERVOUS AT THE START, OF COURSE. All I wanted to do was get on the trail. That last week or two prior to the start is worse than the shootoff. You want to be gone. You want to leave town. You want to be with your team.

I just wanted to finish. I had seen the country, but not from the back of a sled. That's all I wanted to do: Get from Anchorage to Nome in one piece.

The first day was horrible — icy winds, the lakes were slippery. We were dressed in our coldest-weather gear. I was three times as big as I usually am. I'm five-foot-two and weigh 110 pounds. I wore three layers of long underwear and bundled warmer clothes on top. I walked like the Pillsbury Doughboy.

I got out of Wasilla OK and made it to Big Lake, but at Big Lake I lost my team.

It was dark. Most of the trail markers were blown away. So there were no markers and in parts of the trail crossing Big Lake — which is like this maze of ice roads — you have to cross a road and the natural instinct is for the dogs to want to go down the largest trail, or the widest trail.

At one point my dogs turned down the widest trail, which was one of the ice roads. I tried getting my team back onto the trail but there was no way I could. So off they went. I went running after the team yelling, "Misty, Misty!" to my lead dog. Waddling along.

There was no way to set a snow hook because of the glare ice but I whoa'd them to a stop. I thought I had them calmed down.

I tiptoed up to the front to grab the leader and pull her back over the snow berm onto the trail. I was in deep snow up to my waist, hanging onto the lines. They were pulling me horizontal on the ground. I had to let go and I thought, "Well, my last hope is to grab the sled as it comes by." To no avail. I couldn't grab the sled. There they went!

All that work and it could be over. I'm not going to be able to go on. I'm going to lose my dogs. And you start thinking money — how much money is running away at Big Lake.

So you've got all this adrenaline and you think you've got this great, big, wonderful adventure in front of you and it's like a bomb has dropped. After screaming for the dogs I was just hoarse. I got back to the checkpoint and found an official and we went to look for the team. Forty-five minutes later, by chance, the team came trotting up behind us.

It was warm that year. We had to stop during the day and let the dogs rest because it was too warm. We were into the 40s and 50s and when it's warm like that the dogs don't do well. It's better to let them stop and rest in the sun — the musher, too — and then you can run straight through the night. Dogs run best at night anyway.

Jamie Nelson was following, driving with Mike Madden, on the way to Iditarod, when Madden got sick. Jerry Austin, Mitch Brazin, Linwood Fielder and I were an hour or so behind them.

All of us were rookies except Jerry. We were the leading rookies at that time. I got there maybe thirty minutes after Mike had fallen off his sled. I came on him first, then Mitch and Jerry and Linwood were there. Jamie was kneeling over Mike saying, "I don't know what's wrong. He's not getting up."

It was Jerry Austin who immediately said, "OK, everybody, let's just pull off." And in two minutes all four of us pulled our teams off the trail, huddled around Mike, and began first aid. We looked at his wound. (Earlier Madden had cut himself accidently.) We checked to make sure there weren't any red lines going up the leg — blood poisoning.

At that point he was coherent, saying he was thirsty, saying he couldn't move, obviously a sick boy. All of us were concerned.

We got him off the trail, built a fire, got him into some warm sleeping bags, then made a decision to send a couple of teams ahead to Iditarod for help. Jerry and Linwood took Mike's team. Eighteen hours later they came back with a helicopter.

That night, Mike became delirious. He was saying, "Put me in the building," and there was no building. And "I'll have the coffee now," but there was no coffee. He had trouble eating. We guessed that somehow he had salmonella or some poisoning to his system.

Our main objective was to keep him warm because it was thirty below zero. We had little toothpick trees for firewood.

ERIC MUEHLING/FAIRBANKS DAILY NEWS-MINER

A youngster in Anvik pets a lead dog from one of the many Iditarod teams that pass through the Yukon River village.

This is as far away from Anchorage and Nome as you can get, in no-man's country, between Ophir and Iditarod. Ophir is just a tent.

My main objective was to get water and electrolytes into him. I had a Thermos full of water. And luckily, there was a straw connected to one of those juice boxes, still attached. I told Mike, "You will take just one or two sips of this water at least every thirty minutes. It's really important, or you're going to be sicker." He agreed. He took a bit of bread and fell asleep again.

Thirty minutes later, his lips were parched, but he didn't want water. I forced him to take some. I came back later and he pushed me away. For almost ten hours, he refused any liquid and got worse. He got the shakes. Bernie Willis came along early in the morning and helped us because we were getting tired. We'd been up all night. This is seven days into the race. Mike had our warm gear and I remember Jamie Nelson and I sitting around the fire, shaking and hoping that help would come soon.

Our hopes and dreams for rookie of the year were dissolved. But I sleep better at night knowing that I helped save the life of a fellow musher rather than having selfish reasons for not stopping to help.

The doctor who touched down with the helicopter said, "Well, Mike, thank goodness for friends like this because another two hours and you wouldn't have been here." Another two hours and he would have been … gone.

By Unalakleet, we heard Mike was OK. He was at the finish line with tears in his eyes to thank each of the people who helped him. He knew exactly who we were, and he and his father were there to greet us.

They had a beautiful Iditarod Good Samaritan Award made for us. And the other mushers voted to give us the Good Sportsmanship Award. I think what we did and the feeling we have means more to us than some rookie-of-the-year award.

"THE CHECKPOINTS" (1984 poster) was dedicated to the checkpoints along the trail.

Joe Garnie says he had no reason to be worried about survival when he spent eighteen hours looking for his dogs in a snowstorm in 1991.

CHAPTER 11:
JOE GARNIE

J OE GARNIE, THIRTY-EIGHT, lives in the Matanuska-Susitna Valley town of Willow with his wife, artist Penny Ann Cross, and their three daughters. Garnie grew up in Teller on the barren, wind-swept Arctic Coast. Only recently has he lived near trees and in Willow, he marvels at the woodsy view from his windows.

Garnie's first Iditarod was in 1978 and his best finishes were third in 1984 and second two years later. Garnie and Libby Riddles were partners raising dogs and racing in 1985 when Riddles won.

In 1986, when Garnie predicted an 11-day winning time, the Iditarod record was 12 days, 15 hours and 11 days seemed improbable. Garnie was right. However, it was Susan Butcher, not Garnie, who set the new record of 11 days, 15 hours, 6 minutes. Garnie finished less than an hour behind her.

In 1991, Garnie had a dramatic adventure on the trail when he lost his team and spent eighteen hours in a raging snowstorm looking for his dogs.

I WAS IN EIGHTH PLACE when I lost my team heading to Koyuk. I figure the way my team was going, I should have come in, at worst, fifth place. I'd seen the weather. I'd grown up in it.

In the early 1970s, I walked for seventy-five miles one time, took me five days in a storm that was worse than this one. I was on a snowmachine that broke down. A storm was coming. I was with another guy and we started walking, from Nome to Teller. We kept traveling. No food either. I figured it's got to break sooner or later and when it does break, I'm almost home.

You ain't going to die. You've got to know how to survive out there. You can get killed going around the corner in New York. A city slicker would know how to survive there. I wouldn't. But I can walk across Alaska for five days knowing I ain't gonna die.

With my friend, I was eating enough snow to keep going. You can't gobble down snow. You melt enough to stay hydrated. We were digging holes. We'd both get in one sleeping bag. The temperature was worse than minus 20.

So when I lost my team on the Iditarod I knew I wasn't going to die. I was going to walk to Elim.

Losing my team was a screwup. I had about fifteen different lies dreamed up by the time I got to Elim, but I had to tell the truth. I just didn't put my snow hook in, going down to that shelter cabin between Koyuk and Elim.

It was getting dark and starting to snow, but it wasn't storming. I got to a fork in the trail and it was obvious that they went back together, but I was feeling good because I was in striking distance of fifth place or fourth. I wanted to be on the hard, main trail, the one with markers, and I ran down there to take a look and I kept going a little farther and a little farther. And I hadn't put my snow hook in. When I came back, my team was barreling down the other trail.

Somewhere they turned around and went back toward Koyuk, because I was walking on the trail and I never saw any sign of them. Then the storm came on. All of a sudden it started blowing. No tracks. The wind came up. I camped there over-night without trying to walk. It was senseless because I had only one set of headlamp batteries and they were getting weak. No food, no nothing. And I didn't have mittens, just gloves, and a pair of Sorels. But it wasn't that cold. It was minus twenty but it ain't that cold if you've got good gear on. I camped there over-night and just dug in. I had stood some pieces of snow up and made a drift. I used my hands. I lay there and let it drift right over me, at least a foot of snow. You want to lay face down, and you dig a hole out in front of your face so you've got some air.

The next day I kept walking and in the storm I walked past the cabin. Could have been by a few feet. Walked by it and wound up at the other cabins down the trail. I found a fisherman's cabin. I stayed a couple hours and melted some snow to drink.

I heard some snowmachines, but they went by. I heard another one and waved him down. We searched for my dogs on a snowmachine all day. Then I got another snowmachine to Elim.

I walked about eighteen hours altogether, with stops. I must have walked ten, fifteen miles. I came in twenty-third. It was disheartening. The only thing I could think of through the whole deal was the dogs. After two days, I was scared I would never find them.

I came in third in 1984. I should have won that year. Susan Butcher beat me by a few minutes. Dean Osmar won that year by two hours. I'd been traveling with Osmar the whole race, from Rohn on. I quit thinking. I rolled into Elim behind Osmar. He stayed there for only thirty minutes. I stayed four hours when I should have gone straight through. That was a mistake. You can't kick yourself in the rear hard enough.

I was still learning about being competitive. Four hours. I watered my dogs and took a nap. Of course, you can't say you would have won. It's just the way it happened.

The next year Libby Riddles won with the exact same team. The dogs were good. They had a year's experience. They were primed.

I was satisfied with that race in 1986. At the banquet, when I drew my number, all I said was, "I'll see you guys in Nome in eleven days." I wish I could get a copy of all the articles where people called me several different things for predicting an eleven-day race. Very competitive mushers said it couldn't be done, wouldn't be done. And the press hit me for blowing off steam because my partner, Libby, had won the year before so I had to try to build myself up.

A record. I had my mind set. We were going to pound it out.

They were special dogs. I never even brought them into the village until they were nine months old. I kept them loose. I'd tie them at night, but every day, at two months old, I had them running fifteen miles. By the time they were four to five months old, I was running them thirty miles. There was nothing that could run with them. They were a unit. They grew up together, they were all the same age and they all had the exact same miles from the time they were born. In 1986, they were four years old, right in their prime.

I was first out of Nikolai, first into McGrath. I figured I was going to set the pace from there on. It would have been a hell of a lot faster if I hadn't screwed up by losing the trail out of McGrath. I lost about six hours. I took off at five in the morning, hot to go. First in, first out, ready to start setting that eleven-day pace. The trail makes a forty-five-degree turn up a riverbank. It was daybreak, and I went down a well-traveled trail. It might have been the mail trail. I missed that little turn and kept going.

I was timing myself. I should have been to Takotna. I turned them around and when I got to Takotna, I was back in the pack again. From first place. I figure I went an extra forty miles. Lots of time lost.

Everything I'd worked for the whole year, I'd just thrown out the door. I sat there and watered my dogs and that was the lowest I felt in the whole race. But I made up my mind I was still going to win. A lot of people already had written me off.

I grabbed my sled and turned it upside down. Everything that was an extra got canned. By Kaltag I decided to put the press back on. I knew I'd taxed my dogs extra hard, but they were good and could handle it.

If you've got a good connection with your dogs, you're a part of them and they're a part of you. They're an extension of your arm. If you feel from down deep, those dogs will feel it. We all focus as one mind.

From Kaltag on I led all the way to Safety, twenty-two miles out of Nome. Then Susan Butcher got ahead of me.

Susan had a little more dog left than me. I could see she had more steam. That was a long ride, those last couple hours, knowing I wasn't going to win. I wasn't emotional, I was tired. In fact, I got sick and was doubled over my handlebars going over the hills there. I don't know if it was from working hard, but I had unbelievable stomach cramps. I was in terrible pain.

Second isn't winning. You might as well be in the back of the pack. It's good for the record, but it doesn't do much for you. It pays the dog-food bill. It makes you feel you can win. It isn't anybody else's fault. Everybody else made the right turn. I just wasn't ready to win.

What made me feel the best is that we did it in eleven days. That was the most satisfying part. Everybody who doubted eleven days had to eat their words.

I definitely still want to win. It's hard to say how long I'm going to race. But I was born with dogs. We've always had dogs. All my parents and grandparents had dogs in the yard. I'll probably have the dogs 'til I die.

"A GOAL ACHIEVED" (1986 poster) was dedicated to the women mushers.

Mary Shields, first woman to finish the Iditarod, got a cool reception from skeptical race officials when she called to sign up in 1974.

CHAPTER 12:
MARY SHIELDS

*W*OMEN COMPETING IN, AND WINNING, the Iditarod Sled Dog Race are taken for granted today. But it wasn't always so.

Mary Shields, forty-seven, of Fairbanks, was the first woman to finish the Iditarod. She completed the 1974 race in twenty-third place, just ahead of Lolly Medley. Her time: 28 days, 18 hours, 56 minutes.

Shields never entered the Iditarod again. However, she has raced the one-thousand-mile Yukon Quest race between Fairbanks and Whitehorse, Yukon Territory and in 1991 she competed in the Hope '91 International Sled Dog Race from Nome, Alaska to Anadyr in the Soviet Far East.

Shields, originally from a suburb of Milwaukee, Wis., is an author who gives sled-dog demonstrations on the banks of the Tanana River each summer for passengers from the sternwheeler Discovery. She loves to mush her dogs on long winter camping trips.

*D*URING THE WINTER OF 1973, my husband John and I went on a Christmas trip to Tanana with my dogs and we broke trail about every inch of the way. Coming home, a lot of trail was drifted and we did more snowshoeing. So when I heard of the Iditarod, a thousand miles of broken trail sounded like a wonderful opportunity to see more country.

In the late 1960s, I lived by myself in a little cabin about halfway between Anchorage and Fairbanks along the Alaska Railroad. I learned how to use an ax and a saw. Some friends from Fairbanks came down in October, 1969 to see if I was still alive. They suggested that I use a few sled dogs to help pull in the firewood and to haul the water. They went back to Fairbanks and sent down three old sled dogs and a sled and a pile of dog food. There was a little sign on the sled that said, "Dear Mary, there's nothing to it. Just put the dogs in front of the sled." It was a little harder than that, but eventually I got 'em harnessed up and learned how to do it.

That spring, I took them into McKinley Park and went fifteen miles out to the Sanctuary River. I felt like I was going to the North Pole. I thought that was adventuresome. I had a wonderful time.

I had gone on short trips, but when I look back now at the level of competency I had before the Iditarod, I realize I was pretty green. I think I wore blue jeans the whole way. And a sweater and corduroy kuspuk and shoepacks. It's incredible that I made it, looking back. But when you're young and foolish I guess you can get through anything.

I owned only six dogs, so I bought two more dogs because you needed a minimum of eight to start the race. I trained them around Fairbanks.

My neighborhood had a potluck dinner and kids brought their piggybanks out and they raised money. I think it cost me $700 to run the race, total.

When I called the Iditarod to sign up they sounded skeptical. They asked what I'd done and I hadn't done much. They

VLADIMIR VINITZKI

Mary Shields and her team of huskies train near Fairbanks.

said, "Well, you can come and start if you want to." I got the feeling they didn't take me seriously.

At the start, I was nervous. Anchorage was a big city and I didn't like being in Anchorage. I didn't like having to go up in front of all those people and pull out a number.

I remember a few nervous tears welling up at the start. I wasn't scared, I was just overwhelmed. I was saying good-bye to John. That was part of it.

We started at the Tudor Track. I remember people standing along a fence and someone hollered, "You better turn around now, you'll never make it." That he would tell me I wouldn't make it meant for sure I was going to.

The first stretch wasn't bad. No big storms or anything. When we crossed Ptarmigan Pass we hit a bad storm. I remember going out and meeting seven teams that had turned around — it was too windy. We went back and spent twenty-four hours at Rainy Pass Lodge.

I was prepared for the weather. Most people weren't. They had emergency rations flown in and everyone was complaining, "The race committee has to come and rescue us and bring food!" I thought, "That's not what this race is about." I thought we were supposed to be out here doing it on our own, not complaining that we want someone to break trail for us. I was carrying what I needed to take care of my dog team and I was disappointed that other people were traveling so light. It seemed they should know better than to think the weather was always going to be clear.

I got the impression that other mushers didn't take me seriously because I was a woman, and they didn't particularly want to be seen traveling with me because that meant they weren't doing so well. People were nice, but I got the impression they were embarrassed to be going at my speed.

At Shaktoolik, I remember pulling in and a bunch of teams taking off, and the checker saying, "Well, that's strange. They were going to spend the night here, and then you pulled in and they all took off."

The race was new and the villages were eager to have you. I remember coming into Nulato to cheering. I asked what was the big deal. They told me they were doing a lot of betting. I guess every time Lolly Medley and I got to a checkpoint the women would make money because the men had bet that we would drop out at the first or second checkpoint.

That was when I realized women were watching what I was doing. I remember leaving Nulato and thinking that some of those women were riding along in the sled with me, that I was not racing just for myself. That gave me encouragement during some hard times along the trail.

Near the end of the race I had made a little goal: I wanted to beat Lolly Medley. We both stopped in Safety, and I thought we said we'd stay for two hours, or four hours, or some length of time. We'd get some sleep. I remember waking up and realizing she'd left before whatever this agreed time was, and I didn't know how long she had been gone.

That made me mad, so I wanted to catch her if I could. I don't know what happened between Safety and Nome. I remember being on the trail, knowing she had left ahead of me, and then seeing cars up on the road. So I gee'd my dogs up there 'til I got up to the road and they thought I was Lolly. I said, "No, she's ahead of me somewhere." And they said, "Look, there's a headlamp." And there she was out on the ice behind me. I don't know how I got past her.

I got into Nome about three o'clock in the morning. The fire siren was on and four-hundred to five-hundred people — it looked like a lot for that time of day — cheered me in. And they had that banner across the finish line: "You've come a long way, baby!" They had quite a celebration. They had the mayor's wife welcome me instead of the mayor and the disc jockey's wife interviewed me instead of the disc jockey.

At the time it didn't seem like any big deal. I'm a little embarrassed that people make a fuss over it.

"DESERVING THE BEST OF CARE" (1985 poster) showed a musher putting booties on his leader on the Farewell Burn.

Terry Adkins has won the John Beargrease Sled Dog Marathon in Minnesota but after seventeen tries is still waiting for his first Iditarod win.

CHAPTER 13:
TERRY ADKINS

*J*UST WHEN HE FIGURES he's seen it all on the Iditarod, something else happens to Terry Adkins. Maybe that's why he can't seem to get enough of the race.

Adkins, forty-eight, of Sand Coulee, Mont., has mushed in seventeen races, all but two. That's more than anyone else except race founder Joe Redington. Adkins didn't compete in the 1973 and 1975 races, although he went along as a veterinarian in 1973. At the time he was stationed at Elmendorf Air Force Base in Anchorage. Later, Adkins was transferred out of Alaska but continued to return every year for the race. Adkins retired from the Air Force in 1988 as a lieutenant colonel.

Adkins finished ninteenth in 1974, his debut as a competitor, and ninteenth in 1991, a race he hoped to win. That year Adkins was coming off a victory in the five-hundred-mile John Beargrease Sled Dog Marathon in Minnesota, where he set a course record. His best Iditarod finish was eighth in 1984.

In 1974, musher Herbie Nayokpuk of Shishmaref gave Adkins a dog, Patsy, and nearly two decades later Adkins still runs dogs from the bloodline.

NINETEEN-SEVENTY-FOUR WAS going to be my one and only attempt at the Iditarod. I started with twelve dogs and most of them were either rejects from other teams or dogs right out of the dog pound. I took all twelve all the way to Nome.

The Iditarod grows on you. I want to win it before I quit. I do think if I win I'll quit. There are other enjoyable races — the Alpirod, the John Beargrease — where you can party, sleep in a warm bed and have a hot meal. The Iditarod, you have to work. I kept a log once showing that in thirteen days of mushing, I slept nineteen hours.

The first Iditarod is always the most interesting. Two checkers in Shirley Lake talked me into spending the night there so I could have blueberry pancakes and bacon for breakfast. I could have gone on that night and probably started out with the lead group the next morning.

The pancakes were good, but the delay threw me into a storm at the top of Ptarmigan Pass. Five of us were traveling together and we had to spend the night out in the pass. That was the years before the cold-weather gear. I was in Air Force parkas and hand-me-down whatevers.

That first year and 1991 were the worst years for weather. In 1991 we had three major storms. I was lucky enough to be out in all three of them. Looking at the pictures of us after the race, it looked like we all went three or four rounds with Mike Tyson.

In that 1974 race I traveled with Tim White the rest of the way to Nome from Rainy Pass. I know we went shopping in a couple of the villages. I would buy the peanut butter and he would buy the bread. I think we had some Canadian-made jam, too.

Tim was running six dogs. He would leave a checkpoint quicker than me and I'd usually catch him. Then his dogs would smell the smoke from a village and he'd pass me.

That was the year Mary Shields and Lolly Medley were the first women in the race. Tim didn't want to get beat by the women, so he was in a hurry to leave Koyuk. There was a grader sitting in the middle of the road by the airstrip. On one side there was six feet of clearance. On the other side there was two feet. My leader, Oscar, right out of the Anchorage dog pound, decided he wanted to go on the two-foot side and I got the sled hung up.

Then the dogs decided they wanted to go into this Eskimo cabin and they all got in the entryway. I got them out and I couldn't find the trail. It's midnight. It was cold and no one was around and the only person I could find in Koyuk was a drunk. I put him on the sled and after about an hour he put me on the trail.

I went fifteen miles and the dogs didn't want to go anymore. I lay there and watched the northern lights. Eventually, I made good time into Elim, where I found out that Tim had gotten lost and spent the night in a graveyard near Koyuk. Later, he got run over by a snowmachine outside of Safety. He got to Nome, but with the assistance of a snowmobile. I gave him a trophy with a snowmachine on it. Tim and I have been good friends ever since.

After my second Iditarod, I changed from an adventurer to a racer. In 1983, I thought I had a shot at at the championship after winning the Montana Governor's Cup. It was not to be. I scratched at Topkok Mountain when my team quit on me. Blood tests later showed every dog was clinically anemic. The trail had been mismarked coming out of Grayling. I figure I lost five or six hours on that loop.

In 1991, I had a team I thought could win. I got to Ophir in first place, then had to break trail. When you're breaking trail you're obviously going slower than the teams behind you. Then the team got a virus at the end of the Yukon River. I dropped five dogs.

You've got to take care of your dogs. If something happens to any of them it always affects a musher. It was just a maintenance race after that. I think 1991 was the only year I ever trained. I had longer, more quality miles. Everything else was just playing with dogs. The first Iditarod I had a total of 429 miles on the team. I had four-thousand miles on the 1991 team before I went to the Beargrease in January. I trained at six-thousand feet or higher. I felt I could win when I went to the Iditarod, but I didn't factor in the weather.

There are four factors to winning a dog race. The first is genetics. The second is nutrition. The third is training or

Two Siberian huskies sleep in harness in front of the Rohn Roadhouse checkpoint.

conditioning. The fourth is luck.

In the 1988 race, I was hit by a middle-ear infection. I was dizzy. I scratched because I couldn't stand up.

In 1980 or '81, I'm not sure which, I was going down the Dalzell Gorge. Most of the time the creek is running, but there's shelf ice. I came around this curve and my leader went out on the ice. I saw the trail ... but I stepped off the sled, and slipped. My feet went above my head. I went straight into the water. It takes your breath away, I'll tell you that.

It was twenty-something degrees, but I completely stripped. So I was mooning Ernie Baumgartner when he came around the curve. All I had on were my bunny boots.

I don't remember the year, but during one Iditarod, somewhere right after Knik, I went around this curve and there were two women standing there. One of them was quite attractive. All of a sudden, she turns around and moons me. I kept going, but I did yell that the the almanac didn't say anything about there being a full moon.

Later I learned it happened to other mushers, too. It turns out the other woman was the mother and she bet the girl $5 a musher that she wouldn't moon us.

Things happen on the Iditarod. One year at Shell Lake it was raining. One guy had a raincoat. The rest of us were wearing garbage bags. I never expected to run the Iditarod in volcanic ash either. I broke my hand in the Dalzell Gorge. I think the Iditarod is the unexpected.

You forget the frostbite and you forget the heartaches and you just remember the good parts. If I died tomorrow I'd have had a full life just running the Iditarod.

"ALONE ON THE CREST OF YOUR DREAMS" (1983 poster) shows a lonely stretch of trail near Rainy Pass.

DeeDee Jonrowe has seen severe weather conditions that would discourage less determined mushers but she keeps coming back to run again.

CHAPTER 14:

DEEDEE JONROWE

*D*EEDEE JONROWE, THIRTY-SEVEN, is a college basketball player turned Iditarod musher.

Although she is small, standing just five-foot-two, she played college basketball while attending the University of Alaska Fairbanks. Later, Jonrowe began dog mushing when she lived in Bethel in Southwest Alaska, where she worked for the state Department of Fish and Game. Her size has not been a handicap.

Jonrowe lives in Willow, Alaska, with her husband Mike. She has nearly one-hundred dogs in her lot. Jonrowe has raced in nine Iditarods and won Minnesota's John Beargrease Sled Dog Marathon in record time in 1989.

As a youngster, part of a military family, Jonrowe lived in Germany, Greece, Ethiopia and Okinawa. An animal lover all her life, she had two horses and thirty-five guinea pigs when the family moved to Virginia. In addition to raising sled dogs, Jonrowe also has an avid interest in show cats.

*T*HIS WAS MY NINTH IDITAROD and we've had storms in the past, but the 1991 race had the longest stretch of storms that I've ever raced in.

Leaving Ophir was a challenge because it was not a broken trail and it was ninety miles to Iditarod. We went out about fifteen miles where we broke off the main trapper trail, and ended up in bad, bad, deep, heavy snow. Even breaking it with snowshoes was difficult.

For me, that was the changing point in the race. We went about three hours and set up camp and decided we might as well wait for everybody. We would take turns breaking trail and make the best of a bad situation.

It was a long stretch to Iditarod and I should not have broken as much trail as I did. At that time my leader, Johnnie, was doing an excellent job. I also was making my decision based on how much food I had in my sled. It's kind of a Catch 22. You don't want a heavy sled. It makes it that much more difficult for the dogs to pull through the snow. And yet you know it's going to be a long, slow trip and you have to carry enough food. If you're fortunate enough to be driving a big dog team — I had fifteen or sixteen dogs — you need quite a bit of dog food to keep going.

It was a struggle. I was tired. Had that been the only stormy section of the trail it wouldn't have been too bad. But that was just the beginning. It stormed all the way up the Yukon River. It was blowing hard enough that if you were a couple of hundred feet behind the team in front of you, you were breaking trail again.

It was particularly bad between Grayling and Blackburn and then on into Eagle Island, where we would have been able to break the competition loose in normal years, down into packs of five or ten. But we still had twenty-six teams stacked on top of each other. It looked like the start of the race.

The storms defined the 1991 race and probably changed the outcome. The fastest team didn't necessarily win. I know our team was one of the fastest, yet we paid a toll for all the trailbreaking we did.

In 1985, they kept freezing the race to get supplies in and everyone fell back and regrouped and rested their teams. That wasn't the case in 1991. We just kept plugging away, doing the best we could. To make the situation worse, we got on the coast and the storms came and the temperatures were low — thirty, forty below and a windchill of nearly one-hundred below. And colder. This is real intense. It's difficult to cook dog food outside, boil water at one-hundred below zero.

In 1990, when I finished in a storm, it was twenty above and blowing sixty and seventy. In the 1991 race, all the way from Shaktoolik to Koyuk, it was blowing sixty and seventy and it was thirty-three below.

I was tired of the wind blowing. And I was tired of not being able to maneuver buttons or zippers and things like that. Normally, if your hands get damp, you can still put on your liners and do things. Well, those liners, if they got the least bit damp, were hard as rock. So you kept changing gloves and if they had any moisture in them they were frozen solid.

You let the ruff get away from your cheeks and nose and they're frozen. All of us suffered frostbite, with the exception of Kate Persons. Mine was on my cheeks and nose and it wasn't nearly so bad as some people's. There was nothing you could do about it. You were glad because you didn't feel it anymore.

It wasn't as much fun as, say, mushing on a warm, sunny, clear day but it separates the dog teams. I finished seventh. I think the conditions favored experience.

Tim Osmar runs up a draw outside the Rohn checkpoint with a part of the cloud-covered Alaska range in the background.

Tim Osmar, a commercial fisherman when he isn't training, has raced sled dogs his whole life and is determined to win the Iditarod.

CHAPTER 15:
TIM OSMAR

*T*IM OSMAR, TWENTY-FIVE, lives a unique outdoor lifestyle, even by Alaska standards. He lives with his wife, Tawny, and two young children in Clam Gulch on the Kenai Peninsula in the heart of Alaska's sport-fishing territory.

In the summer, he is a commercial fisherman with his father, Dean, who lives nearby.

In the off-season, he trains for the Iditarod. He has competed in six races and finished fourth three times. In 1991, Osmar was traveling with the leaders out of White Mountain, seventy-seven miles from the finish in Nome, when a major storm hit and broke up the group. He was forced to retreat to the checkpoint.

Osmar grew up in a dog-mushing household. When he was a boy, his father became interested in the sport and began raising dogs. Dean Osmar won the 1984 Iditarod.

The younger Osmar raced in the Junior Iditarod four times, winning three championships.

I WAS ONLY EIGHTEEN for my first Iditarod in 1985 and the whole race was overwhelming. It was a rough year.

It was stormy. That was the year Libby Riddles won. Right from the start we had freezes. They stopped the race. We had a three-day freeze at Rainy Pass, a freeze at Ophir, too. Both messed up my strategy.

I've been in some storms around Clam Gulch, but it's different when it's in your own home country and you know what's going on. This was my first time out of Shaktoolik and it was flat nothingness for a hundred miles. It was a little better than zero visibility, but my lead dogs were burned out at the time.

I thought I'd have a shot at being up there with the top two or three, or maybe winning — kind of unrealistic. Being a rookie there's just so many things working against you.

It was a humbling race, but it wasn't anything to be ashamed of. Thirteenth was pretty good for a first year. The race throws curves at you. At the time it seemed devastating. Every time I've run, I've come away with more knowledge.

All my races have been satisfying in their own way and I've always been a little mad about something I did wrong. I haven't stopped learning. Susan Butcher's still learning, too. There are so many factors. So many things can happen — weather, wild animals, losing the trail, losing your team. Weather's the main one. If it's a cut-and-dried year, hard, fast trail all the way, no weather, then the person with the best team wins.

If you're warm and dry and everything's going well, it's easy to have a good attitude. If I'm warm and comfortable, even if it's blowing fifty, as long as we're making progress, it's neat. Some-times — I won't deny it — I do hate it. When I'm cold and miserable and it doesn't look like there's any change for a while, you do hate it. But you know it's going to be over eventually.

I was more rested in 1991. You have to have everything as simple as possible. You have to get used to not sleeping. I do it in normal life, too, with fishing and training long hours. Nothing compares to the Iditarod. You just handle it.

You've got enough adrenalin flowing and enough riding on it, if you're into it. Some people can stay up and some people can't, but the people who are consistently in the top ten are good at staying awake.

I could get two hours' sleep, where Susan and Rick might get three or four, if they're a little more efficient and have their act together better. At a checkpoint, you usually don't get much more than an hour. Even if you're there three or four hours, you've got a lot to do. In that four hours you're spending an hour and a half mixing food and feeding dogs, and then you've got to have something to eat yourself, so you get to where there's only one hour left for sleeping.

The area between Kaltag and Unalakleet is my favorite part of the trail — the whole feeling of rolling hills, and some trees, and open meadows. I never have had bad weather through there. You're off the darned Yukon, that's the main thing. You're on your way to the coast.

I've got to win. That would be the turning point in a guy's career, to win the Iditarod. Everything would go well after that. Being able to sell dogs, to get sponsors, to turn a profit. Rick Mackey is still Iditarod champion. It follows you. I know it does.

I know I can do it. It could have happened in 1991 if things had been different. My team was doing excellent. I just didn't have enough dogs. I had eleven dogs and two of them didn't make it. It was too hard on them to keep up.

I don't know if I would have been a musher if my dad hadn't been one. I was ten or eleven when he started getting dogs. But before that we'd get up to Anchorage to watch the start of the Iditarod. We'd watch the Fur Rendezvous on TV and go around and watch the local races. When I was eight, watching a sprint race, I didn't think I'd be running the Iditarod.

I'd come home after school and run every night. I wouldn't do anything else. I was more into it than I am now, more gung ho. When you're young and you're excited about something, you go overboard.

I've had illusions on the trail. Bedsprings over my head, big buildings. Bedsprings hanging from trees, ducking them, looking back and saying, "Oh, it wasn't really there."

Between White Mountain and Safety in 1991 there was a big,

"ALONE. TOGETHER. TEAMWORK STRENGTHENED IN SOLITUDE" (1980 poster) reflects the pain and hardship found on the Iditarod.

old white rabbit. Susan, Joe Runyan and I were running, after we waited for the storm to calm, and there was a rabbit. It looked like Alice in Wonderland. There's no doubt in my mind it was there. I saw it run off.

My most heart-pounding moment was in 1990. I had just left Rohn with a fresh team, ready to cruise with two of my craziest leaders in front.

Suddenly there were buffalo everywhere. One was in the middle of the trail. By the time I got my sled stopped, the lead dog was maybe forty feet from one. It's a winding, narrow trail, and you don't have much warning. He was pretty stubborn.

I haven't measured many buffalo. They're not as tall as a moose, but they're wider and thicker. A thousand pounds, for sure. He took a few steps forward and that got the lead dogs going. I fired a few shots off. I didn't want to shoot at it. I just fired a few rounds up in the air. It didn't do nothin'.

The whole race passed before my eyes. I thought if the dogs

ran into him it would be all over, with those big horns. I was sure he'd do in at least half of them. I mean a moose is one thing. I think that buffalo could be devastating. That's what I was concerned about.

After a few minutes Susan came up behind me and asked what the problem was. She came running up with her red suit on, asking what to do. I said, "I don't know." And she kind of lifted her arms up like, I don't know what to do, either. The buffalo saw that and ran the other way. It was funny.

I wiped the sweat off my brow and took off. You're all shaky, you know, like almost having a car accident.

In the 1991 race, I rested six hours at White Mountain and then we left about three in the morning, into that storm. I returned about eight that morning. It was bad. I could have stayed out there if I'd been more prepared. I had two candy bars, one little bag of fish for my dogs and I had left my bunny boots behind. I still had on these old Sorels a friend in Unalakleet gave me and the insoles were wet. I got really cold.

That was my major mistake. I was uninformed. I didn't take it upon myself to find out what the weather was going to be. It was darned sudden. But still, some people are more knowledgeable than others about what's going to happen. Rick and Martin Buser were ready. And they had better gear, too.

I could have gone on, but I probably would have lost a few toes.

"AS RUGGED AS THE LAND" (1985 poster) honors a lead dog named Bobo
and all other dogs on the Iditarod.

*Jerry Austin considers
the Iditarod a vacation
from operating a fuel
company, guiding
hunters and fishing
commercially for
herring.*

CHAPTER 16:
JERRY AUSTIN

*F*OR JERRY AUSTIN, THE IDITAROD is a vacation — no
phones, no radios, a time to relax.

Austin grew up in Priest Lake, Idaho, and Seattle, and
came to Alaska at age twenty-one after graduating from the
University of Washington. He joined VISTA (Volunteers in
Service to America), which his cousin, Glenn Olds, former
president of Alaska Pacific University, helped organize during
the Kennedy administration.

Austin, forty-four, lives in the historic Bering Sea com-
munity of St. Michael with his wife Clara and their four
children. He has raced in thirteen Iditarods. His first was in
1976 and his best finish was third in 1982. He has finished in
the top ten six times.

When he isn't mushing dogs, Austin operates a fuel
company and a hunting guide service and commercial fishes
for herring. Austin has about sixty dogs in his lot. He and his
wife donate the annual $1,500 prize for the Iditarod's Rookie
of the Year.

IN 1973, WHEN THE FIRST Iditarod was on the radio, I hooked up two dogs and started running them. Everybody wondered if those guys would make it. I decided I was going to do it.

As corny as it sounds I grew up watching Sergeant Preston of the Yukon on TV. I grew up with tales of Alaska. My dad, Walter Austin, owned a company that sold lubricators to the Alaska Railroad. He told me stories about how many bears he saw when he was out fishing.

It took me three years to get dogs together. I got four of the seven dogs that Carl Huntington finished with when he won in 1974. Carl Huntington and his dad Sidney got me hooked. Carl gave me the dogs for nothing. One of those dogs' names was Melissa. That was the only dog in history that won the Iditarod, the North American and the Anchorage Fur Rendezvous World Championship Sled Dog race — all for Carl.

My first Iditarod was in 1976. I finished in the middle, twenty-third out of forty-six. I finished with eight out of twelve dogs. A drunk in Kaltag kicked one of them and broke the dog's leg. It was probably the coldest race ever. That was when I got to meet Rick Swenson and we spent time together and became buddies.

It was seventy-one below at Ophir. Clarence Towarak, myself and one other guy left Ophir. We only went ten or twelve miles and stopped and made a big fire. It was miserable. It snowed almost every day. Seventy-one below, it's dry. You can tell it's at twenty-five below and it feels warm. I've been in everything.

Twice I've cracked a bed on tobaggan sleds at seventy below. One time when I was hunting we had to take frozen ribs out of moose meat and fashion a toboggan bottom out of the ribs. I've done that more than once. You've got to tie them in right. You've got to do something when you're fifty miles from home.

I wanted to do well in the race that first year and I was in the top eight or ten all the way to Koyuk. There, Emmitt Peters told me, "Rest your dogs because it's almost a straight run into

Nome." I didn't rest them as long as the other guys. I ran to
Elim and I just lost all these positions. I was in like twenty-fifth.
I should have listened to Emmitt. He's a village boy and he knows.

My second year I went from twenty-third to ninth. That was
1978. My best finish was in 1982 when I was third. Basically, Rick
Swenson and I broke trail the entire way to Nome. That was
probably the stormiest year. It was one storm after another.
Emmitt Peters was up there. Rick Swenson and Emmitt and I
did the leading.

A whole bunch of us got hung up at White Mountain.
There were thirty-mile-per-hour winds, blown-over trail and the
markers were too far apart. Same old story. As a matter of fact,
there was a picture of Rick and me and Susan Butcher in National Geographic that year. In the picture, the three of us were
all sitting on the checker's bed. We looked like death warmed
over. We looked older than we do now. We looked just terrible.

We stayed there several hours. That was the last race Susan
ran without an outstanding leader. She tried to lead and went
right out on the lake. Her dogs turned off into the driftwood.
That's right at the bottom of the Topkok hills. The wind was
blowing hard. They weren't used to going into the wind. We
went by Safety. It was still stormy. Emmitt was behind us. We
could see him now and then. Rick and I were going side by side.
We were just sitting on our sleds talking about racing down
Front Street. Susan was behind Emmitt.

We couldn't have been more than three miles out when the
weather lifted a little and all of a sudden we saw a dot. Damn, we
said, that must be Susan.

I could kick myself a thousand times for what Rick and I did
all the way to Safety. For nineteen of those miles we just
lollygagged along. We were going to see who had the best leader
after all those miles. And all of a sudden, we got caught. Susan
beat me and she nearly beat Rick.

Probably the most fun I ever had in the Iditarod was traveling with Dewey Halverson and being in front all the way to
Unalakleet in the 1987 race. We were bear guiding together in
the fall of 1986 and came up with a plan.

I'd like to think Dewey and I set the new standard for
running the Iditarod. It used to be that you raced from White

ERIC MUEHLING/FAIRBANKS DAILY NEWS-MIN

A musher pulls off the trail to care for his dogs on a frozen river.

Mountain in to Nome, then it was Unalakleet, then from McGrath. But that year we were distancing people by Skwentna. We went for broke into Rohn. We gained five hours on the average good musher into Rohn. A lot of people burned up their dog teams trying to catch us. We were the first two out of every checkpoint to Unalakleet. If we'd had better dog food, we'd have pulled it off.

I love the Iditarod. It's my vacation. There are no phones, no radios. I relax more on the Iditarod than at any other time of the year. It's easier than commercial fishing.

The worst trouble I ever had was when I was up to my neck in water. It was 1976. We went through Ptarmigan Pass. It's the south fork of the Kuskokwim. You just had to walk your dogs through water up to your waist. The sled would be downstream from you. It's cold water, thirty-two degrees. I slipped and was totally soaked.

I was hypothermic when I got to Rohn. Ken Chase had to pull me over to the fire. It was ten degrees, not real cold out, but that is the most miserable I've ever been in my life. And I've got scars and bullet wounds all over my body. Between Unalakleet and Nome, that's where somebody will get killed on the Iditarod.

Last year, when I was on a training run, there were a couple of polar bears up near my cabin. It's mostly grizzly bears that provide our excitement, though. When I'm mushing in the fall and spring when bears are out, I carry a high-powered rifle.

In July, 1991, my old leader Lightning, who is fourteen years old, went with us up to our cabin. It's forty miles from St. Michael by boat. He took off after a bear and we couldn't find him. We tracked him to where this great big bear was standing in a willow patch and we assumed he was dead. We looked the next day and came back two days later and we figured the bear had nailed him.

Lightning ran fifteen races for me. He was my leader from 1978 to 1989 and was in eight Iditarods. He was never dropped, not once. A great dog.

About ten days later, we stopped back at the cabin and there was Lightning. The bear had swatted him on the shoulder and tore a hole in him, but he was fine. He must have been eating dead walrus or something all that time.

"THE START OF A LONG FRIENDSHIP" (1986 print) was dedicated to
Dennis Corrington, with whom Jon Van Zyle ran in the 1976 race.

Joe Runyan, "the thinking man's musher," has won three major distance races — the Iditarod, the Yukon Quest and Europe's Alpirod.

CHAPTER 17:
JOE RUNYAN

*J*OE RUNYAN, FORTY-THREE, has been called "the thinking man's musher." He is fascinated by outdoor challenges that test the limits of human endurance and has great admiration for people who tackle daunting tasks and who pursue adventure. Runyan is regarded as a scientific musher who studies and interprets past performance charts.

A one-time trapper near Tanana at the confluence of the Yukon and Tanana rivers, Runyan won the 1989 Iditarod and is the only musher to have captured the championships of the Iditarod, the Yukon Quest (in 1985) and the Alpirod (in 1988) race in Europe. He has competed in the Iditarod seven times, finishing four times in the top five.

Runyan, who was born in Ontario, Ore., and raised in nearby Boise, Idaho, lives on a fifteen-acre homestead in Nenana with his wife Sheri, their four children, two horses, doves, swallows, homing pigeons, his sled dogs and an English pointer.

*Y*OU CAN GET LOST ON THE IDITAROD, make a mistake. You don't want to blow it. You can never tell 'til the end who's going to win. That's part of the fun. If you didn't have a little of the unknown, it wouldn't be interesting.

You try to think of everything. The way I usually lay it out is I have a best-case scenario and a worst-case scenario. The way to prepare for this is in the gear you send out. You have one bag that's worst-case scenario, in case you need a lot of extra food, or have big storms. It's difficult to predict a clear trail. Someone will assume the lead, but will be stymied by a trail that's not broken, or weather that stops them. You can't expend too much energy getting the lead without making sure you can maintain it.

So every year's different. That's frustating. In many sports, you get another weekend to try it again. I love watching the NBA finals. They lose one game, they get time to make an adjustment for the next game. In the Iditarod you have to wait a year to make an adjustment.

There's great competition, too. It's obviously a top-heavy race dominated by a couple of individuals. But I think the tide can change. New people are working at it.

Winning gives you credentials, gives you access to companies that want you to endorse their products through the Iditarod. That was helpful. It's good for business, definitely good for dog sales. It lends credibility to the whole operation.

People follow the race and get to know you personally, so when you go into a store or a gas station they recognize you. The Iditarod has a lot of name recognition. It's surprising how well-informed people are. I was on a radio show in Detroit with Charlton Heston, who was interested in the Iditarod and knew all about sled dogs.

I had some apprehension in my first Iditarod in 1983. Most rookies overestimate their possibilities. They can't believe the talent's so good, that the dogs are great. Every year it boggles my mind when I discover a couple of dogs with real athletic talent.

JEFF SCHULTZ

Joe Runyan and his dogs come up the Yukon River bank at Kaltag after a long run down the frozen, wind-swept river.

You're training by yourself and you don't have anything to gauge it against. You might be going nine miles an hour and think you're cooking, and everybody else is going ten. When you get in the race that mile an hour makes a big difference.

I may never be as comfortable being out in the woods as I was at that time. I was living a lifestyle of trapping and fishing on the Yukon. Now I'm older and more accustomed to the benefits of civilization. So now when I hit the trail it's always a bit of a shock.

In most professional sports you have a draft that evens out the playing field. Certain talent goes to the worst team so they can improve. We don't have that in the Iditarod. You get dynasties going and it's hard to do well against them. Now, though, with sponsor interest, there are more people with the freedom to do as well as they can. In the next few years, I think it'll be more competitive.

Now there's enough money and interest that every good dog that's available is probably going to be there at the start of the Iditarod. There's no hidden talent, there's no wonder leader that's undiscovered. Most of the great Iditarod dogs have been identified and people are pursuing those dogs all the time. There's a big telephone network across the continent looking for good dogs. If we get a good, clear trail, I think the record will be broken because the dogs are getting faster.

I get nostalgic. Now it's tarnished, you know, because you think about the prize money and you think about getting a good sponsor. You definitely need the adventurers, the amateurs, the ones who are setting aside a block of their life to do it because it's something they want to do. I hear from people like that all the time, phoning, looking for dogs. It gives a flavor to the race, and you need that flavor to make it a success.

The only place I've been apprehensive on the trail is going from Shaktoolik to Koyuk in 1991. The pack was holed up at a shelter cabin outside of Shaktoolik, and I decided to go on. About halfway to Koyuk my headlamp went out and I started fooling around trying to get it fixed. The wind was so strong, plus there's a lot of spindrift, it gets in your mitts, and I felt my hands getting cold fast.

You're in control, but you know you're tired and a little

dehydrated. Right away I thought, "Oh-oh, I'm going to frost-bite my hands." If you frostbite your hands, you're in trouble. I put them under my armpits fast and managed to heat them up. I burned the tips of my fingers. It was a little uncomfortable the rest of the way. But I'd never had that happen before. It irritated me, but it happened so fast.

It's just like the old-timers say. If you make one little mistake, it can lead to a bigger mistake and a bigger mistake. You always keep that in mind — don't let this thing get out of control. Don't let your fingers get frozen and then get in a jam where you can't zip up your coat and then get in a jam where you're getting cold. Soon you're in a dangerous cycle.

I always knew even before the race that if I got into a dicey position I would turn around and race another day rather than take a chance. You just have to figure out how important it is to you.

"LEAVING RUBY" (1991 print) honors the Yukon River village of Ruby, known for its friendliness and hospitality.

JIM BROWN

Rudy Demoski was a trapper who used a dog sled team for transportation, not racing, when he signed up for the Iditarod in 1974.

CHAPTER 18:
RUDY DEMOSKI

*R*UDY DEMOSKI, FORTY-SEVEN, says racing in the Iditarod these days is different than it used to be when a musher from a small village in the Interior or along the Bering Sea Coast could pull together a team and compete. Now it requires thousands of dollars to be competitive, he believes, and it's tougher for an unknown to break in or to obtain sponsorship.

Demoski, who formerly lived in Anvik on the Yukon River, raced the Iditarod six times, the first time in 1974. He finished fourth that year in the race won by Carl Huntington.

Demoski lives in Wasilla with his family and a team of sprint dogs he inherited from a friend. Those dogs may have a future in sprint races for Demoski or as part of the team of legendary sprint musher George Attla.

THE 1974 IDITAROD WAS the first dog-sled race in my life. My brother-in-law, Ken Chase, raced in 1973 in the first one. It sounded like something I could do. The entry fee was only $200 in those days.

I trained my dogs on a trap line, trying to get them tough for distance. That's all we did. We were trapping the fur-bearing animals — marten, beaver, wolverine, whatever.

I thought it was going to be fun. I had a good dog team. I wasn't worried about the distance. Well, maybe in the back of my head I was a little worried. Strange country. Didn't know what to expect. As soon as I reached the Yukon, from McGrath out to the Yukon, from there I knew everybody into Unalakleet. I had friends and relatives all along the trail.

I never did plan for a race. I just went according to what my dogs could do. You never know what's going to happen to your team. You never could make one specific plan in those days and then try to stick to it. The dog care was different, the food was different. They never had the high-quality foods that they have now, especially out in the villages. In those days, it was just beaver and dried fish. Feed your dogs dried fish and beaver and they went all right.

My first race, I traveled with Warner Vent, who finished second. He taught me all I know about dogs. He gave me suggestions what to do with the dogs. On the trapline, you're stopping all the time to check traps. In a race, you're going steady. You went until your dogs got pooped and then stopped for a while. I did a lot of night traveling. It's cooler.

There was a 130-below wind chill at Ptarmigan Pass. Warner and I were lost three times in one day. I had a good topnotch leader, Cubby. He'd go anyplace I told him to. It was blowing so hard it drifted, and hard drifts, so we just kept going. We passed George Attla three times that day. He knew where he was going because he went there in 1973.

We checked out every opening on the right side of Ptarmigan Pass going toward Hell's Gate. There's Rainy Pass and a couple other passes running out.

Not so good. Sure was cold. Every place that looked like an opening, we'd go that way. Then we'd turn back and catch George Attla's trail and pass him again.

It must have been about forty-five miles. It took us maybe seven, eight hours. Warner and I were in the top seven all the way.

Only two teams were ahead of me after Unalakleet, Carl Huntington and Herbie Nayokpuk. Warner and I started pushing right from Unalakleet and we caught Herbie at Koyuk. I had to camp on the ice that night about ten miles outside Koyuk. I had young dogs in the team and a couple of them folded over on me. It was whiteout, blowing, so I camped there and waited 'til morning.

From Koyuk we had Herbie start ahead of us. We caught him on the ice between Moses Point and Koyuk. It was blowing and snowing wet snow. When we caught Herbie we had to break trail. Herbie knows the country and we don't. He said, "Boy, you're going to have to snowshoe all night because the east wind has blown the ice out and it could break up the ice and drift us out to the ocean."

We got scared. I think Herbie was scared a little too, but I think maybe he lied to us, too, so we'd break trail for him.

When Warner and I got too tired to snowshoe, I dug a hole right beside my sled and put my sleeping bag down. I was so tired in the morning I never felt the four inches of water I was sleeping in. When I woke up you couldn't see anything. The sled's just covered up. It snowed about a foot and a half of wet snow. We had to walk all the way to Elim that day.

I was hoping I could come into Nome on my birthday, but it was a couple days later. I turned thirty on the race.

There was hardly anybody in the street when I got to Nome at six in the morning, but boy, it sure filled up fast. The bars close at five. Everybody was still drunk. The last day I stayed up twenty-eight hours going from Golovin to Nome.

After the 1974 race I always looked forward to March and racing again. It got in my blood.

In the back of my mind, I know I'll race again. I've got to do well, though. I get a little bummed out at the start of the race each year, but I don't have the caliber dogs to be out there competing. And I know it, so I don't miss it so much.

"BEYOND THE UNKNOWN" (1988 print) represents Jon Van Zyle's encounter with spirits on the Yukon River.

Jon Van Zyle was traveling alone at night in 1979 when he heard a strange whispering that turned into laughter, then applause.

CHAPTER 19:
JON VAN ZYLE

*A*N INTERNATIONALLY KNOWN wildife artist, Jon Van Zyle is as closely identified with the Iditarod as any of its champions because as official Iditarod artist he has painted numerous scenes of the race. He has been the creator of the annual Iditarod poster since 1977.

Van Zyle, who says he "paints what I know," gained his familiarity with the Iditarod by competing in it. He raced twice, finishing thirty-third in 1976 and forty-second in 1979.

Van Zyle, forty-nine, lives in Eagle River near Anchorage with his wife Char and six sled dogs. Van Zyle has raised dogs all his life and believes his gravitation towards the Iditarod was natural. A long-time recreational and sprint-race musher, he enjoyed experiencing the wilderness with his huskies.

*R*UNNING THE IDITAROD completely changed my life. It made me aware I could do anything if I put my mind to it.

It's hard to explain. You don't think about the hardships. That's not part of perseverance, not if you live that way. The fact that you accomplished the goal, that's the real thing — the heck with perseverance, the heck with what it took to get there. I've always lived the kind of life where physical exertion isn't a tough thing. That's just the way I live. I've always been focused. I never started anything that I couldn't finish.

The country is so vast and the Iditarod race was such a new thing in 1976. There wasn't time to smell the flowers, like you would if you were just mushing. You can't spend the time talking to people. But I had to look around, to talk with people in the villages, because that's who I am. And if I had allowed myself just to run, then I'd have been cheating myself. And I didn't do the Iditarod to cheat myself.

There was a bad snowstorm and nine or ten of us who had been traveling together were pinned down between Kaltag and Unalakleet for two-and-a-half days. No trail.

We probably got to know that country between Kaltag and Unalakleet as intimately as anybody who has traveled there. We were in a large valley and we went from one side of that valley to the other, and back, trying to locate the trail. We were never "lost." We were searching. The guy I was with, Dennis Corrington, had a spyglass. We had been snowshoeing in front of the dogs for days, never finding the trail markers. We were standing on this little knoll and he was looking for anything that he could see and that's how we found a marker.

It was frustrating. When you're traveling with dogs, there's not necessarily a trail, so the dogs I had that year had walked behind me single file while I snowshoed in front of them. They had done their own trailbreaking in snow completely over their heads. They were tough dogs.

Finishing was important. The things that you learn about yourself change you. They make you know who you are. There's a camaraderie with your dogs. You've done something with them. By pushing them harder, you build a stronger bond. There is a sense of accomplishment.

About four seconds after I finished the race, I said, "Gee, I don't want to do this again." And from then on my life was incomplete. So I ran again in '79 and to be honest with you it was not the same.

I had a better dog team. I had a tough, slogging, there's-nothing-we-can't-tackle dog team the first year. In 1979, I had a faster dog team because I trained them faster. But the race had changed, as far as the camaraderie was concerned. More intense competition.

Some metaphysical things happened, though. I had a vision, I guess you would call it. And I know I wasn't hallucinating because I had slept three or four hours prior to that. The dogs were feeling great, I was feeling great, we were just loping along between Blackburn and Kaltag. It was maybe three or four o'clock in the morning.

As I got closer to this area, I heard "whisper, whisper, whisper" — talking. A murmuring. And it got louder and louder and more distinct. That went into laughter. Nothing raucous, not "Ho, ho, ho" — just nice laughter. Like someone was having a good time. And that went down — cue the laughter down and cue up the applause. And as I got closer to this spot, wherever this spot is, the applause started. You could hear the applause a long time — for three, four, five minutes. It got loud and then it died off.

Nobody was there. I wasn't dreaming. I was awake. When I came back I did a painting about it. A priest called. He said, "I used to be on the Yukon River and I know where the spot is." He said he'd tell me all about it. We never met. But I did a bit of research on it and I think in that area there's a place called Massacre Island. Because the river is so wide, I mean, there could be fourteen Massacre islands in a four-mile stretch. There was a massacre there. Some missionaries were killed ... and I think those are the people. They were watching a bunch of crazy dog mushers. And they gave me a little round of applause. I think it was neat. The priest told me, "You're not the first person who's heard these people."

"BOBO" (1991 print) captures the memory of the Siberian husky who was Jon Van Zyle's best friend for fifteen years.

Another neat thing happened in 1979 going down the Post River. I left Rohn in late afternoon, stopped and fed my dogs. I had not slept in approximately two days. But this "thing" has nothing to do with a hallucination. I don't practice an organized religion. I don't practice any religion but I consider myself religious and quite spiritual.

I fed my dogs and went on. The Post River had open water with thin, dark glare ice and no moon. My headlamp battery was dead. There were lots of holes, and because it was so dark, I couldn't see far enough ahead to call my leaders around them. We nearly slid into a couple of openings in the ice. That' when I decided to walk up front with my leaders. I turned my sled on its side to slow the team. A spiritual person had told me if I ever felt as if I was in dire straits, I should ask for protection from the White Light. I did. We made it around this mile or two of dangerous trail. It was scary — not a comfortable situation.

A little farther down the trail I stopped and was feeding dogs when this musher caught me. He said something about being able to see me on the river. And I said, "How did you do that? I didn't have a headlamp." He said, "I was behind you quite a ways and all of a sudden, it was like somebody had turned a light on you."

It was the White Light.

"EARLY MORNING LIGHT" (1989 poster) shows that wolves are among the spectators along the Iditarod Trail.

JEFF SCHULTZ

*Jacques and Claire
Philip of France are
regular competitors in
both the the Iditarod
Sled Dog Race and
Europe's Alpirod race.*

CHAPTER 20:
JACQUES & CLAIRE PHILIP

*T*HE IDITAROD HAS ATTRACTED international attention
and competitors from throughout the world. Most of the
foreigners come to Alaska, run once, and never are seen again.
But a French couple, who first came north on a vacation, keep
coming back again and again to run the Iditarod.

Jacques Philip, thirty-five, and his wife Claire, thirty-
eight, have homes in Willow, Alaska, and in the suburbs of
Paris, France.

Jacques has run the Iditarod six times and Claire twice.
Jacques' best finish was eleventh in 1989. Claire's top finish
was twenty-sixth in 1987. Their first race was 1985, the year
Libby Riddles won. They regularly compete in the Alpirod,
the European dog-mushing stage race that goes through
several countries.

Of all the visiting foreigners who have competed, the
Philips are the most persistent and consistent while retaining
ties to their home country. They bring a unique perspective to
the Iditarod.

*J*ACQUES: THE SLED-DOG SPORT started in France in 1978 or 1979, and that's when I met Claire. She had one Siberian Husky and went to Canada for vacations. I was doing outdoor sports — mountain climbing, sailing. But Claire didn't like that. She liked dogs. So I figured maybe it would be a way to find a new adventure, to go to Canada and Alaska.

We went to the Yukon Territory and traveled through that country. When we went back home we joined the first dog-sled club formed in France. The following summer, in 1979, we went to New York and bought a little camper and drove it to Earl Norris' in Willow, Alaska. We came in the summer and stayed until January.

In that club we joined in France, we were among probably thirty people. Only four or five of us actually were running in races. Year after year it grew, so after a while it got to be rather popular. It was a curiosity.

Claire: At that time we just wanted to learn about mushing dogs.

Jacques: It was a full-time hobby. I was finishing my studies in medicine, but I took one year off to mush dogs. We didn't do anything else. I think it's already more than a hobby when you give up everything — even if you don't think it's forever.

After we went back home, we brought a few more dogs and we ran French races and the limited class in Europe for three years. But the thing is, since we had been in Alaska, we had seen the Iditarod. We had helped Earl Norris train dogs for Martin Buser. We thought we should come back to run it.

We contacted Joe Redington and he helped us. It was 1985. We had a few of our own dogs. A few. Originally, I was going to lease a team from Joe. Finally, he gave us two teams. We leased one and he gave us one for Claire, who wasn't planning to run.

Claire: Joe made me believe in myself. "You can do it and I will help you. I will give you some dogs." I told him, "I don't have any leaders." He said, "Don't worry, you will have a leader to start the race." And he provided me one of the best leaders.

And we both went to Nome that year.

Claire: We were in Knik, living in an old bus. Nothing was easy before the race. Later, we both wanted to do it again. We did it again, in 1987, but that time we were much more organized. We learned a lot. And the year after, we wanted to improve what went wrong the year before and after a few years you realize it's hard to send two teams. Now we're working on one team.

Jacques: After the 1987 race, we bought ten or twelve dogs from Joe and we took them back to France. In the meantime, we had been breeding some Siberians that we left in France, so we had forty to fifty dogs.

Claire: We lived forty miles from Paris. It's not like Alaska. When you are forty miles from town in Alaska you have nobody around. But where we lived, it's crowded and it's always different living in small villages. You have to deal with your neighbors. Nobody knew how many dogs we had because I tried to keep them quiet. And we didn't let anybody come to our place and see what we were doing. We tried to keep our kennel a secret. But everybody knew we had dogs, I'm sure.

Jacques: We were on TV several times, and on radio, and in a few articles about races. People knew us and knew what we were doing. They just didn't know exactly how many dogs we had.

Claire: When you are sleeping, you wake up because they are noisy. You have to run to the kennel, keep them quiet, try to sleep again, and then go back to the kennel. We were exhausted doing that.

When you do the Iditarod once, you feel you can do it again. You feel you're learning. So I think that's mostly why we're doing it over and over again. After the competition you want to improve your place. It's a performance, and you want to try to improve it.

And you get smarter. Maybe your team is not better than the year before, but the fact that you have more experience gives you a better time.

Jacques: We get better every year. The problem is, everybody's getting better every year. It's a young sport and the people like Rick Swenson and Susan Butcher and a few others have fifteen years of experience. It's a sport where you improve slowly.

To get one Iditarod dog takes three or four years. That's one dog. One year you may get three or four good ones out of several litters, but even four good ones doesn't give you a dog team.

I enjoy the camaraderie of the sport. For me it's important. You appreciate the people who are nice to other mushers, who will always be nice to the rookies. When you travel, especially in the top twenty, it's more or less the same people together. But every year or so a rookie sneaks in and you can see the difference of attitude among the mushers. Some of them consider rookies to be nothing. They don't even talk to them. And some consider them like anybody else.

We do the Iditarod because we want to do it. The Alpirod, because we are from Europe, is our main goal because we have a sponsor who also sponsors the Alpirod. If we don't run the Iditarod, we still have a sponsor. If we don't run the Alpirod, we don't have a sponsor.

Right now we wish to continue running the Iditarod. But for me it's not a long-term commitment. Maybe for Joe Redington

ERIC MUEHLING/FAIRBANKS DAILY NEWS-MINER

A musher and team crosses Bering Sea ice near the Safety checkpoint.

it's different. It's his race. He's been doing it all its life. For us, no. We are more committed to sled-dog sport. That's the big difference I can see between us and a lot of people in Alaska. We have a much more general concept of the sport.

Claire: The capital of sled-dog racing is Alaska. You can improve your racing there. You have to run against good mushers. You reach their level or you don't. If we ran only in France we would always be the best because we are more professional than a lot of mushers. What's the point? If we come to Alaska, we have to compete.

Jacques: The goal is to improve, so winning is important. It's part of the goal. But the main thing for me is to have a good time. If you don't have a good time doing it you're in trouble because you can't always succeed in your goals.

Claire: I realized one thing. A lot of people who are winning or who are good in the race will succeed in other fields. They are competitive in their minds. They want to be perfect. They do the best they can. Maybe they won't win, but they will be at a high level, always performing.

Lavon Barve and his team navigate a stretch of the trail on the edge of a glacier thirteen miles north of Rohn.

Lavon Barve amazed race fans in 1991 when he lost his dogs in a storm for eighteen hours but still managed to finish in the money.

CHAPTER 21:
LAVON BARVE

*L*AVON BARVE WAS ONE OF THE FAVORITES in 1991. But as it turned out he was lucky to finish and, some believe, lucky to have survived a harrowing misadventure on the trail.

Traveling with the lead pack between Elim and Golovin, Barve lost the trail and his dogs in a raging storm.

Lacking food and water, and lost in near-zero visibility without shelter, Barve wandered in search of his team for eighteen hours. Finally snowmachiners picked him up on the trail. Then, to everyone's amazement, after warming himself and eating a hearty meal, he found his dogs and completed his run to Nome. He finished seventeenth.

Barve, forty-eight, lives with his family in Wasilla, where the Barves operate a printing shop. His son Lance is a past champion of the Junior Iditarod.

Barve is president of the Iditarod Trail Committee, the official body that oversees the race. He first competed in 1975. His best finish was third in 1990.

*I*TRIED TO PUT MY SNOW HOOK IN. As hard as the ground was, I couldn't get it in. The dogs are over this embankment, I can't go get them, and they won't come back on their own.

So I thought to myself, "Well, I'll walk to the bottom." At the time I thought I was doing the right thing, until I went over that sucker and just kept going and going and going, a quarter-mile, maybe a half-mile. And it was steep, almost steeper than you could walk up.

It was blowing sixty miles per hour right in my face. I made it up the embankment and the dogs were whining all the way, and there was a point where they all started crying and wouldn't go any farther. Now I wonder was that because I had come to the trail? I don't know. Then I lost them.

After pulling the dogs up the embankment, I felt secure that I could leave the dogs and go twenty or thirty feet ahead and come back. Well, that snow blew in before I got back. How long does it take to walk up, turn around, and walk back? I couldn't find the dogs!

I felt confident that I would find them because I'd shut my light off one other time and I could see their silhouette. But I couldn't do that. There was a moon somewhere, I guess, and the snow was blowing. Not much visibility, maybe twelve, fifteen feet.

After walking from midnight to about two o'clock the next day, twelve or fourteen hours later, I was still looking for my team. This storm started to come back in. Something told me to get out of there, that it didn't do any good to keep looking. I headed toward what I thought was a shelter cabin. I never felt scared. I've been out in the woods enough to know you've got to use common sense. What good does it do to be scared?

I was eating snow. I know all the books say you can't eat snow. That does bring the body temperature down — it makes you cooler, no doubt about that — but I was sweating profusely and I had to have liquid in me. You could have wrung my undershirt out. When I got done walking all night, my foam suit had dried out. That suit saved me. If I'd had conventional clothing on, I would have had frostbite.

I knew I didn't have any energy left when the snowmachiners found me. I could have walked on over to Golovin, but I was only moving about one mile an hour. I'd walk two markers or three before I'd stop. Then I'd sit down on the ground and I couldn't get up easily. So I made up my mind I wasn't going to sit down any more. I would sit in a crouch. I was deterioriating.

It doesn't make you feel good to have something like that happen. Some people would have had a "did not finish" tacked onto their name. I knew I'd kick my butt if I didn't finish. I didn't have a lot of fun making the rest of the run.

I was lucky. I came out of it with my dogs. And I was able to get back in the race and finish in the money. If I hadn't had the right clothing, I wouldn't have come out with my fingers.

What I learned from the 1991 race more than anything else — and it's pretty obvious, a hundred people told me — is that you don't leave your dogs. I've had to tell my story one-hundred, two-hundred times, and twenty or thirty people deserved to be punched out, being smart asses.

I knew I had made a mistake.

ERIC MUEHLING/FAIRBANKS DAILY NEWS-MINER

March can bring blizzards or spring–like weather for the home stretch to Nome.

IDITAROD ALMANAC

Q & A

Q. *What is the true distance of the race?*

A. Actually, no one knows for sure because the trail weaves in and out of the natural terrain and its routing often is affected by the weather. Race officials use 1,049 miles as the symbolic distance (Alaska was the 49th state to be admitted to the union) but most estimates suggest the race is at least 1,100 miles long.

Q. *What is the difference between dogs used in distance races and those used in sprint races?*

A. Essentially, the dogs are the same breed — huskies. However, long-distance dogs tend to be larger, in some cases weighing as much as 70 pounds. Sprint dogs will almost always be in the 40-pound range.

Q. *What are "signal whips" and how are they used?*

A. Some mushers carry whips in their sleds and on occasion pull them out and crack them to spur their teams on. They are not used to strike the animals, but rather in conjunction with voice commands to urge the dogs to run faster.

Q. *What kind of food does a musher give his team when he is "snack-ing" them?*

A. The main difference between meal time and snack time on the trail is speed. Full meals of the mushers' own personal mixes, emphasizing proteins such as liver and other nutrients, require that time be spent heating up food. Snacks, in some cases raw salmon or whitefish, can be fed to the dogs quickly on a break.

Q. *Why do officials occasionally stop, or "freeze", the race?*

A. This rarely happens, but in the most famous stoppage of the race in 1985, it occurred because bad weather prevented distribution of the mushers' supplies to checkpoints down the trail. Officials do reserve the right to halt a race because of bad weather, if conditions are considered too dangerous to go on, but those circumstances almost never arise.

In 1991, the storm that hit the front pack leaving White Mountain was so vicious that some talks took place about the possibility of shutting down the race. But it didn't happen.

Q. *How is it that women are able to compete on an equal footing in the sport of dog mushing?*

A. One reason the Iditarod is so popular is that it has female champions in Susan Butcher and Libby Riddles. Women are able to compete and beat men because mushing is not a sport that depends inordinately on physical strength or size. It demands judgment, expertise, wilderness experience, and the ability to train and communicate well with dogs — characteristics possessed both by men and women.

If in some instances, physical strength is an advantage in guiding a sled through difficult terrain, it is thought that being lighter is sometimes an advantage, too, because the dogs will haul less weight.

A DOG RACER'S VOCABULARY

Lead dog: The dog that runs in front of the team pulling the sled. Often the lead dog is the musher's best friend and most reliable dog. Sometimes a pair of dogs will be run in double lead.

Wheel dog: The dogs running in tandem just in front of the sled and at the back of the team.

Swing dogs: They are located just behind the leaders in the team and help steer the sled left or right on command and following the leader's direction.

Team dogs: All of the other dogs in the musher's team.

Hike!: A synonym for "Mush!" The command for the dogs to start running.

Whoa!: The command for the dogs to stop running, although the musher also must apply the brake on the sled.

Gee!: The order for the dogs to turn right.

Haw!: The order for the dogs to turn left.

Trail!: A request by a musher approaching another team for the musher ahead to pull to the side of the trail so he can pass.

Tug line: The line that connects a dog's harness to the tow line.

Tow line: Same as a gang line. The main rope that runs forward through the team from the sled. The dogs are tied into the tow line by their tug lines.

Racing sled: A lightweight wooden frame vehicle that is pulled by the dogs and is the musher's method of transportation across the snow. The frame sits on runners.

Basket: The section of the sled in front of where the musher stands where gear is stowed. If dogs weaken, they are carried in the basket to the next checkpoint.

Brush bow: The semi-circular part of the sled frame that serves as a front bumper.

Toboggan sled: A heavier, sturdier sled, usually used for carrying heavier loads, often over long distances.

BEFORE THE START

Sign-up and entry fee: The entry fee is $1,249 payable in U.S. funds.

Musher qualifications: Mushers must be eighteen years old as of the starting date. Rookie mushers must submit written proof that they have completed a sanctioned race of at least two-hundred miles.

Shipping of food and gear: A minimum of fifty-six pounds of dog food per dog must be distributed among 16 checkpoints along the trail.

Pre-race examinations: All dogs will undergo a physical examination before the race by a veterinarian authorized by the Iditarod Trail Committee. All dogs must have current parvo, rabies and distemper vaccines.

Purse: For the 1992 race, the Iditarod Trail Committee established a $375,000 purse to be distributed as follows:

First place $50,000, second $40,000, third $35,000, fourth $30,000, fifth $25,000, sixth $20,000, seventh $18,000, eighth $17,000, ninth $16,000, tenth $15,000, eleventh $14,000, twelfth $13,000, thirteenth $12,000, fourteenth $11,500, fifteenth $11,000, sixteenth $10,500, seventeenth $10,000, eighteenth $9,500, nineteenth $9,000, twentieth $8,500.

ON THE TRAIL

Mandatory stop: Each musher must take one mandatory 24-hour stop during the race at a time and place most beneficial to the dogs. Each musher also must make one eight-hour stop at White Mountain, where a mandatory veterinary check will be conducted.

Promotional material: The Iditarod Trail Committee may require each musher to carry one container of promotional material, not to exceed five pounds, over the trail.

Sled: Each musher has a choice of his own sled subject to the requirement that some type of sled or toboggan must be drawn. The sled or toboggan must be capable of hauling any injured or fatigued dogs, under cover, plus equipment and food.

Mandatory items: Each musher must have with him or her at all times the following:

1. Proper cold-weather sleeping bag weighing a minimum of five pounds;

2. An ax with a head weighing at least one and three-quarter pounds and a handle at least twenty-two inches long;

3. One pair of snow shoes at least 264 square inches in size;

4. Any promotional material provided by the Iditarod Trail Committee;

5. Eight booties for each dog;

6. One cooker and pot capable of boiling at least three gallons of water.

CARE OF THE DOGS

Qualified dogs: Only northern dog breeds suitable for arctic travel will be permitted to enter the race. Northern breeds will be determined by race officials.

Jurisdiction: Dogs are under the jurisdiction and care of the chief veterinarian and his staff from the time they enter the staging area at the start until seventy-two hours after the team finishes in Nome or are scratched or disqualified.

Dropped dogs: Mushers may drop dogs at designated dog drops. Dogs dropped at checkpoints normally will be moved to the closest dog-collection area or to a location designated by the musher, at the musher's expense.

Size of teams: A musher must have at least seven and no more than twenty dogs on the tow line to start the race. At least five dogs must be on the tow line at all times. No dogs may be added to a team after the start of the race. All dogs must be either on the tow line or in the sled. No dog may be led behind the sled or allowed to run loose.

Switching of dogs: No dogs may be switched between mushers after the start of the race.

Dog care: A musher will be penalized if proper dog care is not maintained. The Iditarod Trail Committee will not tolerate cruel or inhumane treatment of dogs, including any action or inaction that causes preventable pain or suffering to a dog.

Unmanageable teams: Mushers may seek the aid of others to control an unmanageable team.

Driverless teams: Each team and driver must complete the entire race trail and check in at all required locations. A driverless team may be stopped and secured by anyone. The driver may recover his team either on foot, with assistance from another musher or on a mechanical vehicle, and may continue the race.

Motorized vehicles: A musher may not be accompanied by or accept help from any motorized vehicle, including aircraft and snow machines, except when recovering a loose dog or driverless team.

Expired dogs: Any dog that dies on the trail must be taken by the musher to a checkpoint. The musher must report details of the dog's death. An autopsy will be conducted.

Signal devices: Signal whips can be no longer than thirty-six inches. Whips must be kept out of sight of another team. No signal device may be used to adversely affect another team's progress.

Drug use: No injectable, oral or topical drug which may suppress the signs of illness or injury may be used on a dog. No other drugs or other artificial means may be used to drive a dog or cause a dog to perform or attempt to perform beyond its natural ability. Mushers may not inject any substance into their dogs.

REVEL GRIFFIN COLLECTION/UNIVERSITY OF ALASKA ARCHIVES

Togo led Leonhard Seppala's team on the famous serum run to Nome in 1925.

MUSHER CONDUCT

Good Samaritan rule: Other rules aside, no musher may be penalized for aiding another musher in an emergency. Incidents should be explained to race officials at the next checkpoint.

Interference: No musher may tamper with another musher's dogs, food or gear, or interfere in any way with the progress of another team.

Food at checkpoint: Dog food left behind and dog food from scratched and disqualified mushers becomes the property of the Iditarod Trail Committee and may be used at the discretion of race officials.

Passing: When one team approaches to within fifty feet of another team, the team behind shall have the immediate right-of-way on demand. The musher ahead must stop his dogs and hold them to the best of his ability for a maximum of one minute or until the other team has passed, whichever occurs first. The passed team must remain at least fifteen minutes before demanding the trail.

Sportsmanship: Mushers shall conduct themselves in a civil, sportsmanlike manner throughout the race. Abusive treatment of anyone is prohibited.

Parking: Mushers must select a campsite at least ten feet off the race trail so his dogs cannot interfere with other teams — no snacking of dogs in the trail.

Litter: No litter of any kind may be left on the trail, in camps, or in checkpoints.

Use of drugs and alcohol: Use of of illegal drugs as defined by state law or excessive use of alcohol by mushers during the race is prohibited. Mushers are subject to collection of urine samples at any point from the start of the race until one hour after each team's finish in Nome.

Demands for food and shelter: Mushers may not make demands for food and shelter along the trail.

Outside assistance: No musher may receive outside assistance between checkpoints. All care and feeding of dogs will be done only by that team's musher.

No man's land: No man's land is the trail between the Ft. Davis Roadhouse and the official finish line in Nome. Mushers need not relinquish the trail on demand in this area.

ERIC MUEHLING/FAIRBANKS DAILY NEWS-MINER

A weary musher and his dogs sleep along the trail near the Shaktoolik checkpoint.

GENERAL

One musher per team: Only one musher will be permitted per team and that musher must complete the entire race.

Killing of game animals: In the event that an edible big-game animal such as a moose, caribou or buffalo is killed in defense of life or property, the musher must gut the animal when possible. No teams may pass until the animal has been gutted and the musher killing the animal has proceeded.

Finish: An official finish is determined by the nose of the first dog to cross the finish line.

Awards presentation: The awards ceremony at Nome will be held no sooner than the evening following seventy-two hours after the first team crosses the finish line. All mushers who have crossed the finish line up to two hours before the ceremony must be present and the winner must have his lead dog(s) present for recognition.

OFFICIALS & PENALTIES

Penalties: Rule infractions may result in issuance of warnings, monetary penalties, time penalties, censure or disqualifcation. Warnings may be issued by any official. Monetary penalties, censures and time penalties require a majority decision of the three-member panel of race officials appointed by the race marshal. Disqualifications require a unanimous decision of the three-member panel of race officials appointed by the race marshal. The chief veterinarian will be consulted in all cases alleging cruel or inhumane treatment.

"THEY ARE ALL WINNERS" (1982 poster) recognizes that even those mushers who finish last are "winners" in the Iditarod.

ABOUT THE AUTHOR

$\mathcal{A}$ NATIVE OF BOSTON, Lew Freedman, 40, has been sports editor of the Anchorage Daily News since May, 1985. Before moving to Alaska in 1984, he was a staff writer for the Philadelphia Inquirer. He has written prize-winning short fiction, has received dozens of journalism awards, and has been included three times in the Best Sports Stories anthology published annually by Sporting News. In the spring of 1990, he taught in the journalism department at Colorado State University under a teaching fellowship from the Gannett Foundation.

Freedman graduated from Boston University with a degree in journalism and earned a master's degree in international affairs from Alaska Pacific University. He has traveled extensively, visiting all 50 states and in recent years has visited China, the Soviet Union and Africa, writing about those places for his newspaper.

Freedman lives with his wife Donna, a feature writer at the Daily News, and daughter Abby in Anchorage.

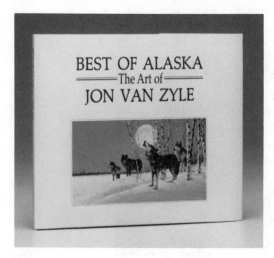

BEST OF ALASKA
The Art of Jon Van Zyle

At last, one of Alaska's most popular artists has published a breathtakingly beautiful coffeetable volume in which he shares 60 of his favorite paintings, offering a personal narrative with each one. His subjects include dogs, wildlife, fishing and wilderness scenes.

Jon Van Zyle is official artist for the annual Iditarod Sled Dog Race and has run the race himself twice. Although his expressive annual portrayals of "The Last Great Race" have earned him an enormous following, and contributed to a growing international reputation as a wildlife artist, his work defies easy categorization. "I paint what I see," he says.

Retail Price: cloth ($29.95) and paper ($19.95)

Size: 80 pages, 9 by 10-1/4: CIP data, 60 full color paintings, 40 black and white reproductions: foreword by Lael Morgan.

ISBN: 0-945397-06-2 (cloth), 1-945397-07-0 (paper)